Mathematics Olympiad

Class 03

BLOOM CAP
Bloom Cap Edu Ventures Pvt. Ltd.

Mathematics Olympiad

Class 03

A must have book for all
Olympiads & Talent Search Exams...

by
Niharika

BLOOM CAP
Bloom Cap Edu Ventures Pvt. Ltd.

Bloom Cap Edu Ventures Pvt. Ltd.

卐 **Administrative & Production Office**

'Ramchhaya' 4577/15, Agarwal Road, Darya Ganj, New Delhi -110002
Tele: 011- 47630600, 43518550

卐 **ISBN :** 978-93-25519-12-1

卐 **PRICE :** ₹100.00

卐 **PO No :** TXT-XX-XXXXXXX-X-XX

For further information about the books log on to
www.bloomcap.org

Follow us on   

Preface

"Future belongs to those Who prepares for it today"

School Olympiads are National & International level competitions conducted by different Government, Non-Government & Educational Organisations with the purpose of making the children ready to face competitive exams. The challenging Questions asked in Olympiads motivate them to learn more & more and bring out the best result with improved academic performance. The Awards & Scholarship offered in Olympiads motivate children to aspire & strive for doing better and emerge out to be the best.

Maths Olympiads

Mathematics is an integral part of all competitive exams be it Aptitude or Commerce or Science. Maths Olympiads are meant to develop Mathematical aptitude in school students. They provide students with an opportunity to master their concepts and comprehend tricky questions effortlessly. Challenging Questions of Maths Olympiads encourage students to develop a logical approach to solve Mathematical Problems.

'Bloom Mathematics Olympiad Study Book Class 3' is a perfect resource to Study & Practice for Olympiad Exams and other National & State Level Talent Search Exams & Other Competitions.

Some Special Features of Bloom Maths Olympiad Study Books are;

- Chapterwise Exercises having different types of Objective Questions at par with the Olympiad Level.
- Detailed Explanation for each question.
- Olympiad Pattern Practice Sets at the end.

This book is prepared by Expert Panel with the utmost care, still if you have any suggestions regarding its improvement, then feel free to contact us at olympiads@bloomcap.org. We will try to inculcate your suggestions in the further editions.

Contents

Numbers

1. The length of which bridge has '2' at the hundred's place?

(a) 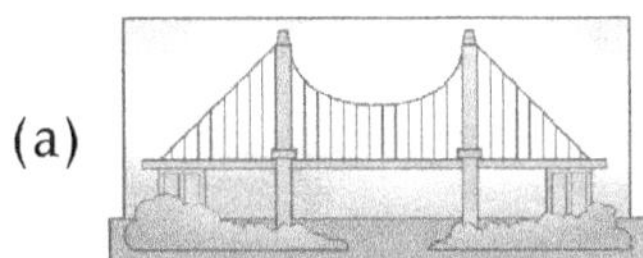

2740 m

(b) 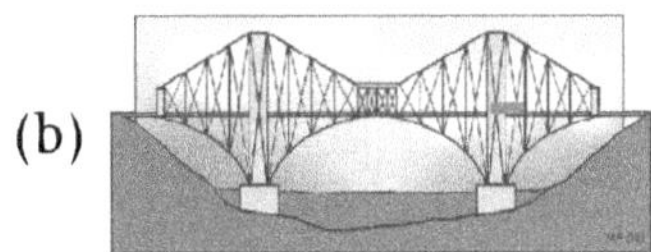

2730 m

(c) 

1261 m

(d) 

2022 m

2. Deepa likes the following type of numbers as shwon in box.

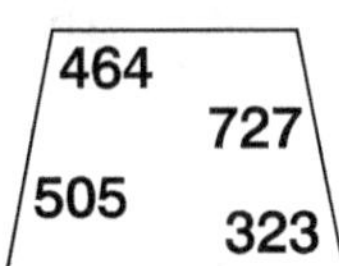

Which the following numbers will she like?

(a) 462   (b) 522
(c) 449   (d) 696

3. Which place value will determine the larger number among the two?

    9763   9736

(a) Ones   (b) Thousand
(c) Hundreds   (d) Tens

4. Look at the given abacus carefully. If two more beads are added to the hundred's bar, then the number it will show now is

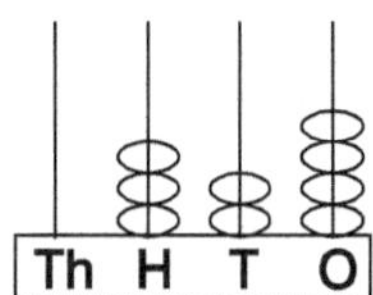

(a) 1228   (b) 524
(c) 1344   (d) 346

5. DBD Bank collected four bags with different number of coins. The number of coins in each bag has been indicated by a sentence given below

A

Predecessor of smallest
4-digit number

B

Successor of greatest
3-digit number

C

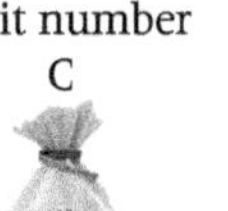

Successor of smallest
4-digit even number

D

Predecessor of greatest
4-digit odd number

Which bag has the greatest number of coins?
(a) B   (b) D
(c) A   (d) C

6. Kim entered a number on a calculator as shown below

What is the number entered by Kim?
(a) 7 hundred 9 tens 0 ones 2 thousand
(b) 70 tens 9 ones 0 hundred
(c) 7 thousand 20 tens 90 hundred
(d) 7 thousand 2 hundred 90 ones

7. A pizza parlour delivered nine thousand eight hundred seventy six number of pizzas in a week. What is the number of pizza written in expanded form?
(a) $9 + 8 + 7 + 6$
(b) $9000 + 80 + 7 + 6$
(c) $900 + 8000 + 70 + 60$
(d) $9000 + 800 + 70 + 6$

8. Match the following columns :

Column A	Column B
A.))) 200 + 70 + 9 ▷	1. 2079
B.))) 2000 + 700 + 90 ▷	2. 2790
C.))) 200 + 9 ▷	3. 279
D.))) 2000 + 70 + 9 ▷	4. 209

```
    A  B  C  D        A  B  C  D
(a) 3  2  4  1   (b)  1  2  3  4
(c) 2  3  1  4   (d)  4  3  1  2
```

9. If ▯▯▯▯ = 1000
         ▯▯▯ = 100
         ▯▯ = 10
         ▯ = 1,

then the given picture represents

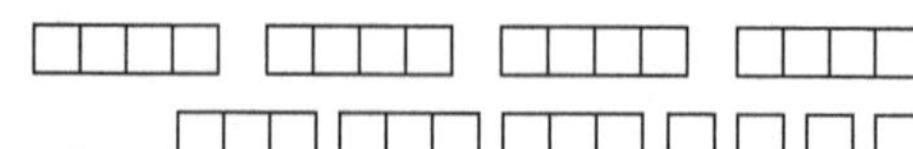

(a) 4321   (b) 4320
(c) 4304   (d) 4324

10. Fill in the blanks.

A. 236   B. 263
C. 504   D. 10001
E. 540   F. 999
G. 405   H. 9999

1. 50 tens + 40 ones is equal to ....

2. Predecessor of the least 5-digit number is ....

3. The number having '0' in tens place, 4 in hundred's place, 5 in ones place is ....

4. If ▯ is 1, then

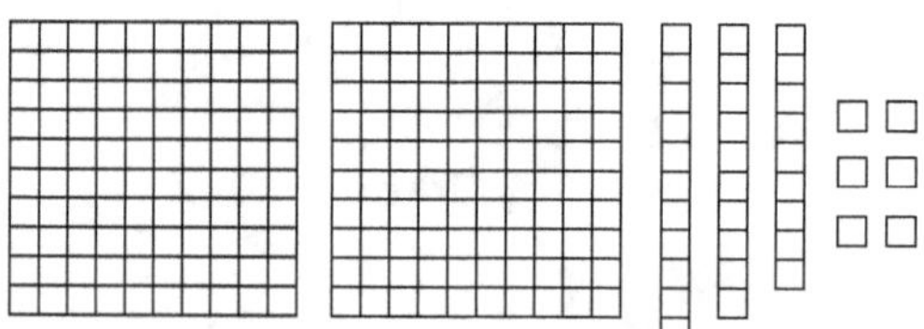

   is equal to ....

```
     1   2   3   4          1   2   3   4
(a) C   D   F   B   (b) E   H   G   A
(c) G   F   C   B   (d) None of these
```

11. Randish put odd number of balls in even number of pots. Among the following options, choose the most possible combination.

(a) 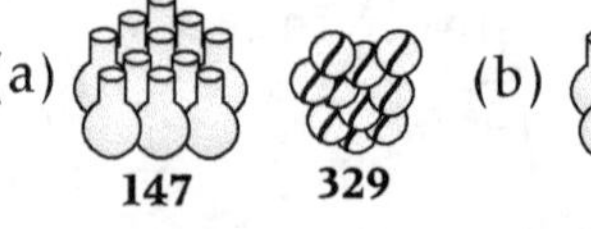

(b) 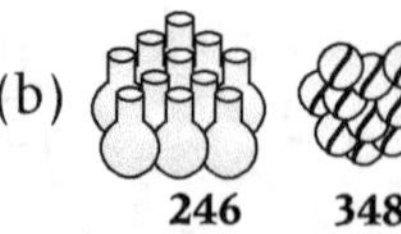

(c) 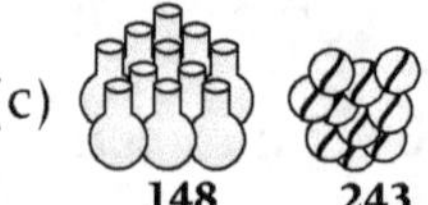

(d) 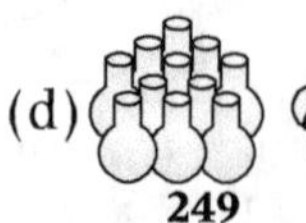

12. If hundred's place digit and unit's place digit is interchanged in each house number, then whose house has an even number in its address?

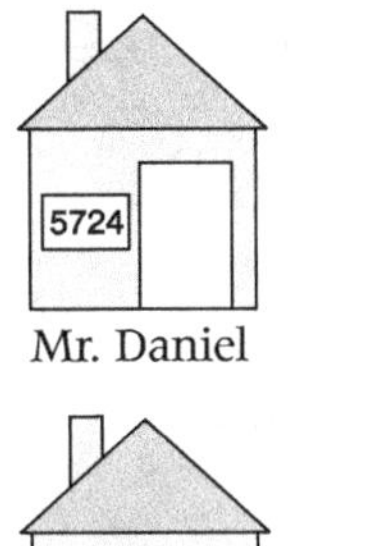

Mr. Daniel

Mr. Addison

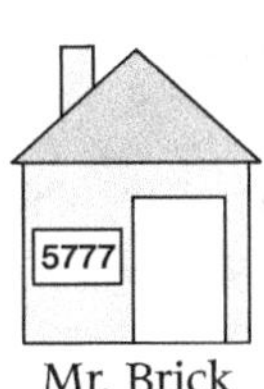

Mr. Brick

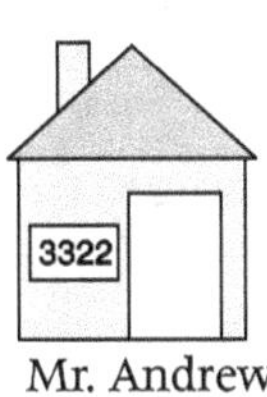

Mr. Andrew

(a) Mr. Daniel   (b) Mr. Addison
(c) Mr. Brick   (d) Mr. Andrew

13. State 'T' for true and 'F' for false.
  1. The smallest three-digit odd number is 999.
  2. 3000 the number shown on the digital board is equal to 30 tens.
  3. The place value of 3 in eight thousand two hundred thirty four is tens.
  4. 1000 + 1 is the greatest three-digit odd number.

	1	2	3	4		1	2	3	4
(a)	F	F	T	F	(b)	T	F	T	T
(c)	F	F	F	T	(d)	T	T	T	F

14. Identify the number.

I am an odd number.

My tens digit is the greatest one digit number.

My hundreds digit is one more than ones digit.

My thousand digit is 2 less than tens digits.

(a) 8493   (b) 6932
(c) 6428   (d) 7493

15. Mahanta scored 1876 marks in her class 3rd result while Shampy scored 1654 marks. Mandy's score is not less than Shampy's score and not greater than Mahanta's score, What could not be Mandy's score from the given numbers?
(a) 1856   (b) 1692
(c) 1776   (d) 1653

16. Read the following statements and mark the option having greatest number in it.
(a) Total length of Indian coastline is 7517 km
(b) An year has about 8760 h
(c) A ten year old child has lived for about 3653 days
(d) An African elephant weighs of about 5500 kg

17. Four friends are playing video games. Their scores are given below

Andy   Ruby

Rizuk   Dondi

Who scored the second highest points?
(a) Dondi (b) Rizuk (c) Andy (d) Ruby

18. Marshal wants to arranged the almirahs in his show room in ascending order of their prices.

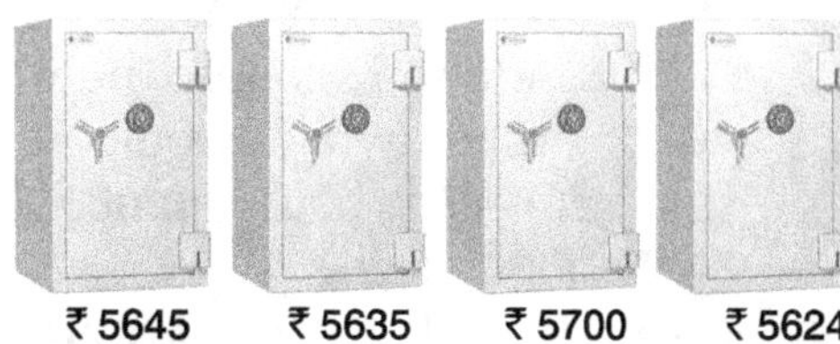

What would be the correct order of arrangement of almirahs?
(a) ₹ 5645 < ₹ 5635 < ₹ 5624 < ₹ 5700
(b) ₹ 5700 < ₹ 5624 < ₹ 5635 < ₹ 5645
(c) ₹ 5624 < ₹ 5635 < ₹ 5645 < ₹ 5700
(d) ₹ 5700 < ₹ 5645 < ₹ 5635 < ₹ 5624

19. Which of the following sets of numbers arranged in ascending order?
(a) 972, 975, 979, 789, 987, 1256
(b) 1320, 1322, 1327, 1237, 1373
(c) 9876, 9768, 9678, 8976, 8796, 6879
(d) 1320, 1451, 7912, 9568, 9658

20. Markew spilled ink drops on his homework sheet as shown below:

A. 562 > 5 ● 2   B. 385 < 38 ●

C. 472 = ● 72

Which digits must be written to make the above sentences true?

	A B C		A B C
(a)	5 6 3	(b)	7 5 4
(c)	2 4 5	(d)	4 7 4

21. The cost of four skirts bought by Mary is

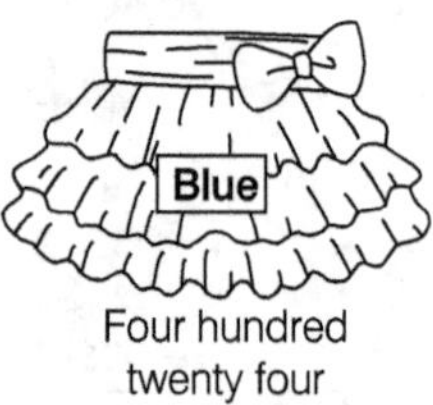

Four hundred twenty four

One thousand two hundred forty

Three hundred two

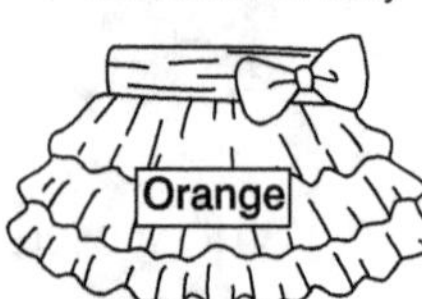

Two hundred ninety nine

Which colour skirt is the cheapest?
(a) Green   (b) Pink
(c) Orange   (d) Blue

22. If Mr. Addison's house number is 6013 , then what would be the smallest 4-digit house number formed by the above digits?
(a) 6013 (b) 1036 (c) 1063 (d) 3016

23. Four students put their favourite number on abacus.

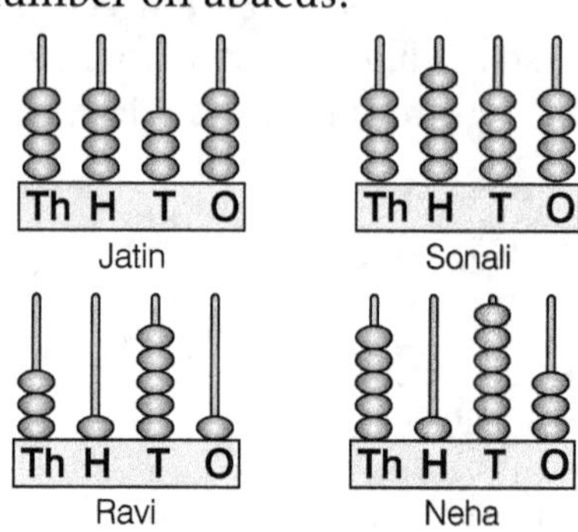

Arrange the students in descending order of their favourite numbers.
(a) Neha, Sonali, Ravi, Jatin
(b) Jatin, Neha, Sonali, Ravi
(c) Neha, Sonali, Jatin, Ravi
(d) Sonali, Ravi, Jatin, Neha

24. $ABCD$ is a 4-digit number such that $A + B + D$ is 9. A is two times of C and B is two times of D. If A, B, C and D are all different digits. Find $ABCD$ as a 4-digit number.
(a) 6231   (b) 2363
(c) 4821   (d) 5212

25. Two trains are carrying different number of passengers.

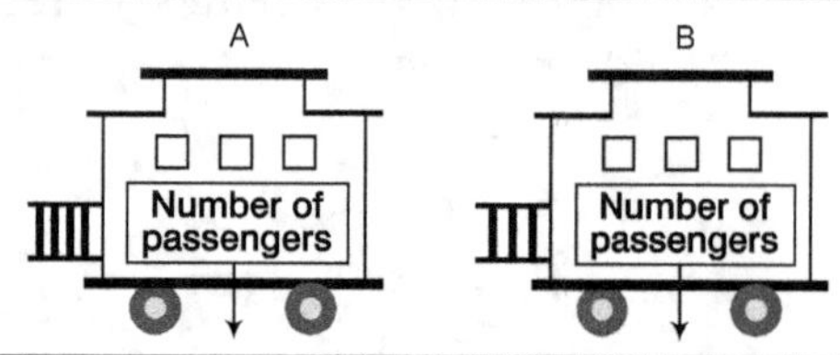

I have a 3 in my ones place. My ten's digit is 3 more than my hundred's digit. My hundred's digit is 2 more than my ones digit.

I have a 2 in my tens place. My hundreds digit is 2 less than my ones digit. My ones digit is 4 more than my ten's digit.

Which train is carrying more number of passengers?
(a) A   (b) B
(c) Cannot say   (d) None of these

Addition and Subtraction

1. Add the $3724 + 4397$. Which of the following number is in the hundred's place of the resulting addition?
   (a) 100   (b) 2
   (c) 0   (d) 1

2. Which of the following option gives the answer when smallest 4-digit number is subtracted from greatest 4-digit number formed the given numbers.

   7, 6, 9, 2
   (a) 8037   (b) 7038
   (c) 7083   (d) 7183

3. Find the missing digit :
   $349 + 4\_0 = 779$
   (a) 0   (b) 1
   (c) 3   (d) 2

4. People in United Kingdom(UK) measure long distances in kilometres than in miles. Michelle and her family drove from London to Swindon last weekend by the following route.

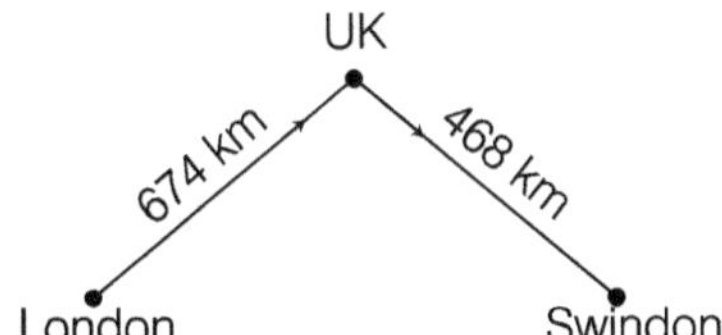

   What is the distance covered by them?
   (a) 1142 km
   (b) 1100 km
   (c) 1050 km
   (d) 1150 km

5. The sum of 1629 and 7465 is ______ .
   (a) Nine thousand Nine hundred four.
   (b) Nine thousand Ninety four.
   (c) Six thousand three hundred thirty four.
   (d) Nine thousand three hundred seventy eight.

6. In a car parking, there were 873 blue cars and 1317 white cars. There were 127 more red cars than blue cars. How many cars were there in the car parking?
   (a) 1390
   (b) 3090
   (c) 3190
   (d) 3291

7. Amantha uses a mental strategy to solve the problem $158 + 243$. In Step 1, she groups hundreds together. In Step 2, she groups tens together and in Step 3, she groups her ones together, as shown below:

Step 1	Step 2	Step 3
100	50	8
+ 200	+ 40	+ 3
300	90	11

Which should be Amantha's next step to complete her strategy?

(a) $300 + 90 + 11$

(b) $300 + 90$

(c) $300 + 11$

(d) $90 + 11$

8. If $7 + 2 = 9$,

$70 + 20 = 90$,

$700 + \text{😊} = 900$,

$\text{😊} + 2000 = 9000$,

then the sum of $\text{😊} + \text{😊}$ is

(a) 6200

(b) 7200

(c) 4820

(d) 5020

9. What number should be subtracted from the least five-digit number to get the greatest four-digit number?

(a) 1000   (b) 111

(c) 11   (d) 1

10. There are 2100 men and 2450 women in a village. Find the population of women more than men in village.

(a) 450   (b) 350

(c) 250   (d) 500

11. Find the missing numbers :

340, 310, ..., 250, ...

        (i)   (ii)

(a) 270, 210   (b) 280, 220
    (i)   (ii)   (i)   (ii)

(c) 270, 220   (d) 210, 280
    (i)   (ii)   (i)   (ii)

12. If the digit at hundred's place is changed with the digit at one's place, then what is the difference between new number and original number shown by the abacus?

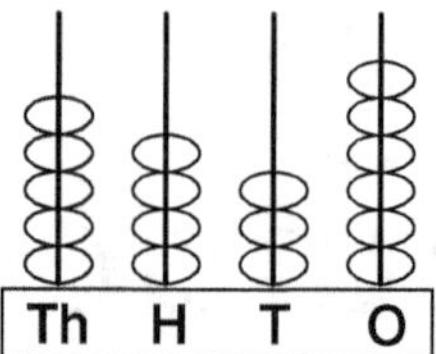

(a) 198   (b) 203

(c) 191   (d) 195

13. Ruby went to the market. She bought vegetables for ₹ 240. She gave ₹ 2000 note to the shopkeeper. How much change will the shopkeeper return?

(a) ₹ 1760

(b) ₹ 1670

(c) ₹ 1270

(d) ₹ 1450

14. Jack cycled from point B to C. He then cycled from point C to point A. How far did he cycled together?

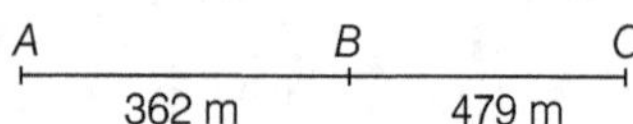

(a) 941 m

(b) 841 m

(c) 1017 m

(d) 1320 m

15. Find the value of $(A - B)$.

$$\boxed{A}\,7\,8\,2$$
$$-\ 4\,9\,\boxed{B}\,1$$
$$\overline{1\,8\,2\,1}$$

(a) 1   (b) 6

(c) 2   (d) 0

16. Find the value of $(A+D)-(B+C)$.

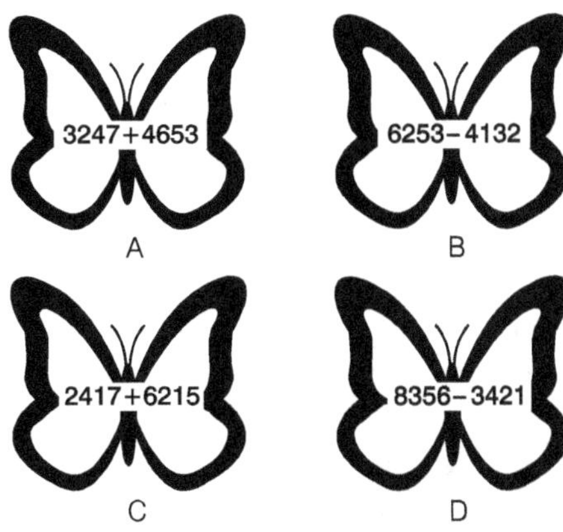

(a) 2182

(b) 2280

(c) 2082

(d) 2820

17. What number is covered by the flower?

If $\bigcirc + \triangle = 30,$

$\triangle + \triangle = 40$

and $\triangle + \square = 50,$

then $\bigcirc + \square = $ ✿

(a) 10   (b) 20

(c) 30   (d) 40

18. 630 ml of water is poured into a fish tank containing 490 ml of water. If 120 ml of water spilled out from the tank. What is the volume of water in the tank?

(a) 900 ml

(b) 1000 ml

(c) 800 ml

(d) 1950 ml

19. What is the difference between the place value of digit 7 and the place value of digit 2 in the number 7592?

(a) 7000

(b) 6998

(c) 7998

(d) 4672

20. Aslam has 324 stamps. This is 124 more than the stamps Ravi has. How many stamps does Ravi have?

(a) 206

(b) 216

(c) 312

(d) 200

Chapter

03

Multiplication and Division

1. Which number sentence describes the number of stars in drawing below?

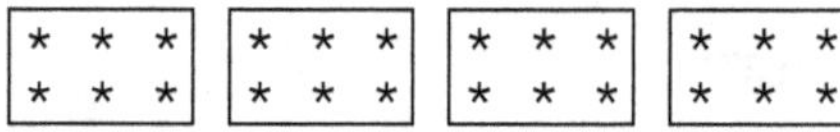

   (a) $6 \times 3 = 18$ (b) $6 \times 4 = 24$
   (c) $3 \times 12 = 36$ (d) $4 \times 4 = 16$

2. Rubal grouped 15 counters in 2 different ways to represent a basic fact.

   1. ⬭ ⬭ ⬭ ⬭ ⬭

   2. ⬭ ⬭ ⬭

   Which number sentence represents these related facts?

   (a) $5 \times 3 = 3 \times 5$ (b) $5 \times 3 = 5 \times 5$
   (c) $3 + 5 = 5 \times 3$ (d) $5 + 3 = 3 + 5$

3. Samantha is having a birthday party at her place. She prepared rainbow coloured cupcakes sets for desserts. If she made 7 sets each for the 7 colours of the rainbow and each set has 6 cupcakes, how many cupcakes did she prepare in total?

   (a) 7   (b) 42
   (c) 19   (d) 294

4. A reporter wrote a report, which is published in a newspaper. It has 21 words in each line. If the report has 62 lines, How many words are there in the report?

   (a) 1302
   (b) 1203
   (c) 1361
   (d) 1412

5. Jolly's class students contributed ₹ 3 each to buy chart paper. How much amount of money is collected by his class, if the number of students in the class is given by the figure shown below?

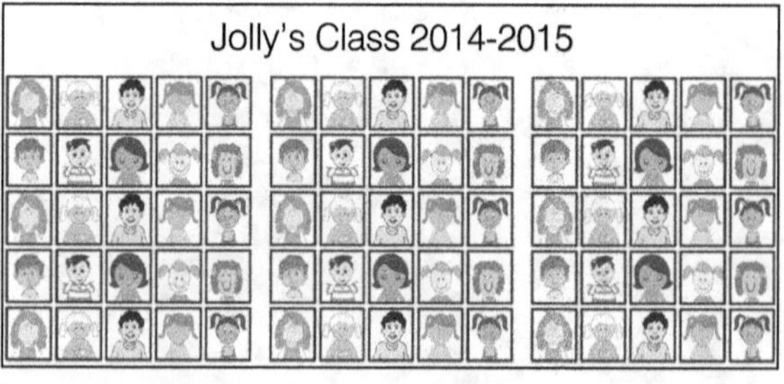

   (a) ₹ 225   (b) ₹ 75
   (c) ₹ 25   (d) ₹ 125

6. 108 beads are used to make a Japamala. How many beads are needed to make 15 such Japamala?

(a) 1260   (b) 1540
(c) 1620   (d) 1360

7. Harshit built 5 bird houses each day for a week (1 week = 7 days). Her dog knocked over and broke 2 of the bird houses. How many bird houses are left unbroken?
(a) $7 + 5 - 2$
(b) $(7 \times 2) - 5$
(c) $(7 - 2) \times 5$
(d) $(7 \times 5) - 2$

8. Suzene has 80 pencils. She gives all of the pencils to her 10 friends. Each friend gets the same number of pencils. Find how many pencils were given to each friend.
(a) $80 + 10$
(b) 80×10
(c) $80 - 10$
(d) $80 \div 10$

9. Eric collected different stamps. He promised his sister to share with her one of his collections given below

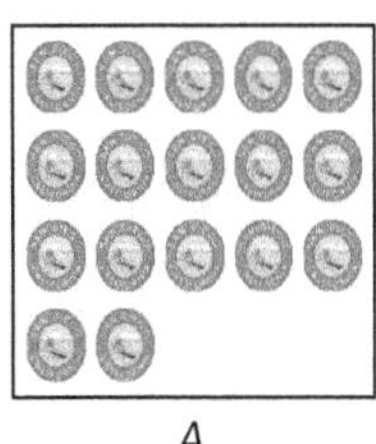

A

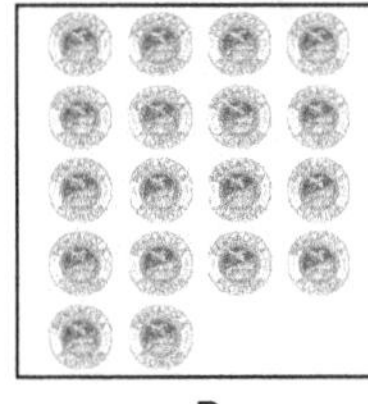

B

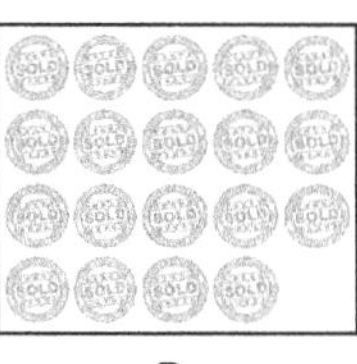

C   *D*

Which collection of stamps can Eric share equally with his sister?
(a) A   (b) B
(c) C   (d) D

10. Mr. Andrew wrote the following problem on blackboard.

> Ann had 14 pens.
> The product of number of Ann's and Marshall's pens is equal to 56.
> Marshall had Δ number of pens.

Which number sentence matches the number of pens Marshall had?
(a) $14 \times 56 = \Delta$ (b) $14 \div 56 = \Delta$
(c) $56 \div 14 = \Delta$ (d) $56 + 14 = \Delta$

11. The product of two numbers is 2979. If one of the numbers is 9, the difference between the two numbers is ………. .
(a) 322   (b) 340
(c) 349   (d) 331

12. There are 4 shelves to keep apples in the fruit shop of Ms. Bendick. Each shelf has room for 15 apples. If Ms. Bendick has 72 apples, how many apples will not be able to fit on the shelves?
(a) 72   (b) 60
(c) 15   (d) 12

13. A group of students went for a trip to a place which was 300 miles away. 10 miles before the halfway point they stopped to have lunch. How many miles do they still have to go?
(a) 240 miles   (b) 140 miles
(c) 160 miles   (d) 270 miles

14. Find the missing number.

$$7\overline{)489}(\,\square$$
$$\underline{42}$$
$$69$$
$$\underline{63}$$
$$6$$

(a) 69   (b) 70

(c) 79   (d) 60

15. Which of the following is incorrect?

(a) $115 \div 5$ is less than 115×0
(b) $480 \div 6$ is equal to 16×5
(c) $12 \times 5 = 12 + 12 + 12 + 12 + 12$
(d) 65×1 is equal to 1×65

16. State 'T' for true or 'F' for false.

1. 2×7 is equal to 7×7.
2. $8 \div 4$ is equal to $8 + 8 + 8 + 8$.
3. If $44 \div A = B + 1$, then $A = 4$ and $B = 10$
4. If the given number ends with zero, then we can divide the number by 10.

Codes

	1	2	3	4		1	2	3	4
(a)	T	F	T	F	(b)	F	T	F	T
(c)	T	T	F	F	(d)	F	F	T	T

17. Rohit saves ₹ 1.25 everyday from his pocket money. How much does he save in a month of June?

(a) ₹ 34.75   (b) ₹ 37.5

(c) ₹ 42.55   (d) ₹ 31.5

18. Which one of the following statement is incorrect?

(A) : 12 pairs of socks are 24 socks.
(B) : 5 rainbows have 35 colours
(C) : 8 dice have 45 face
(D) : chess have 32 white/black squares.

(a) (C)   (b) (D)

(c) (A)   (d) (B)

19. Linda's uncle and aunt pay Linda to help them in their work each week.

> They pay ₹ 12 each week to mow their yard.
>
> They pay her ₹ 2 each week to wash their dog.

Which expression shows how much Linda's uncle and aunt will pay her in 7 weeks?

(a) $(12 + 7) + (12 \times 2)$
(b) $(2 \times 7) + 12$
(c) $(12 \times 7) + (2 \times 7)$
(d) $(12 + 7) \times (2 + 7)$

20. Observe the given multiplication

$$7\boxed{P}9$$
$$\underline{\times\ 6}$$
$$43\boxed{Q}\,4$$

What is the sum of P + Q ?

(a) 6   (b) 9

(c) 7   (d) 5

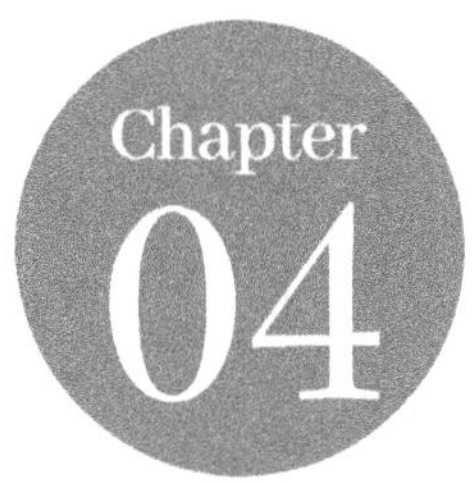

Chapter 04

Fractions

1. What fraction of the given figure is shaded?

   (a) $\dfrac{3}{8}$
   (b) $\dfrac{4}{8}$
   (c) $\dfrac{5}{8}$
   (d) $\dfrac{1}{2}$

2. Which of the given pair is correctly matched with the fraction of shaded parts?

   (a) 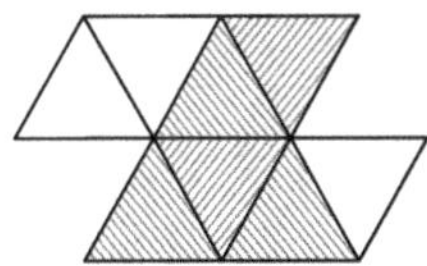 $= \dfrac{1}{2}$

   (b) $= \dfrac{6}{10}$

   (c) $= \dfrac{3}{8}$

   (d) $= \dfrac{4}{16}$

3. How many tenths are there in $\dfrac{7}{10}$?

   (a) 7
   (b) 9
   (c) 3
   (d) 10

4. Which of the following figure sets shows $\dfrac{1}{5} < \dfrac{3}{5}$.

   (a) 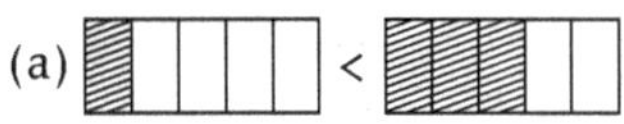 $<$

   (b) 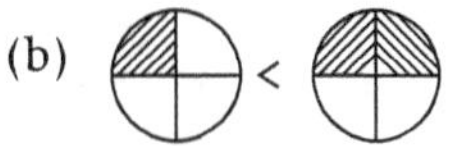 $<$

   (c) 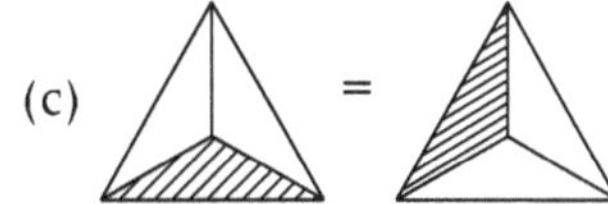 $=$

   (d) 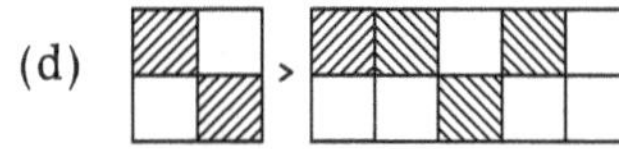 $>$

5. The 5 days weather forecast of a week is given below:

   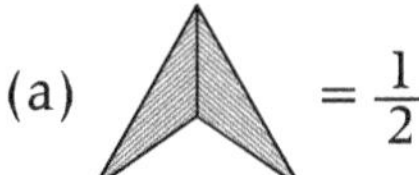

Sunny	Rainy	Rainy	Sunny	Sunny
Monday	Tuesday	Wednesday	Thursday	Friday

   What fraction of days are sunny?

   (a) $\dfrac{2}{5}$
   (b) $\dfrac{1}{5}$
   (c) $\dfrac{3}{5}$
   (d) $\dfrac{4}{5}$

6. Find the equivalent fraction of $\dfrac{1}{3}$ with numerator 7.

   (a) $\dfrac{3}{27}$
   (b) $\dfrac{21}{7}$
   (c) $\dfrac{7}{21}$
   (d) $\dfrac{9}{14}$

7. In the following word, what fraction of letters are made up of more than three straight lines?

NUMERATOR

(a) $\dfrac{1}{9}$ (b) $\dfrac{3}{9}$ (c) $\dfrac{4}{9}$ (d) $\dfrac{2}{9}$

8. Jady had 17 stickers. She gave 4 stickers to Amantha and 6 stickers to Ruby. What fraction of stickers are left with her?

(a) $\dfrac{4}{17}$ (b) $\dfrac{6}{17}$ (c) $\dfrac{10}{17}$ (d) $\dfrac{7}{17}$

9. Kristane bought 30 cupcakes. After eating 6 cakes, she gave $\dfrac{3}{4}$ of the remaining to her sister. What fraction of the cupcakes was left with Kristane?

(a) $\dfrac{10}{30}$ (b) $\dfrac{6}{30}$

(c) $\dfrac{1}{2}$ (d) $\dfrac{20}{30}$

10. One-fourth of the money was spent on buying vegetables. One-half of the money was spent on buying fruits. Another one-fourth of the money was spent on buying grocery products. Which of the following figures shows the money spent on each item?

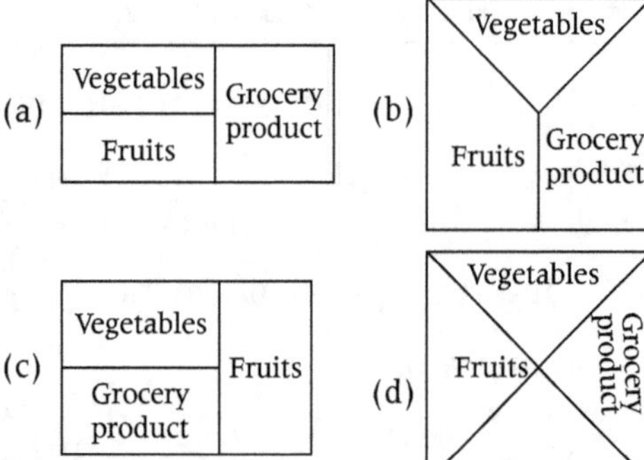

11. State whether true or false.

1. 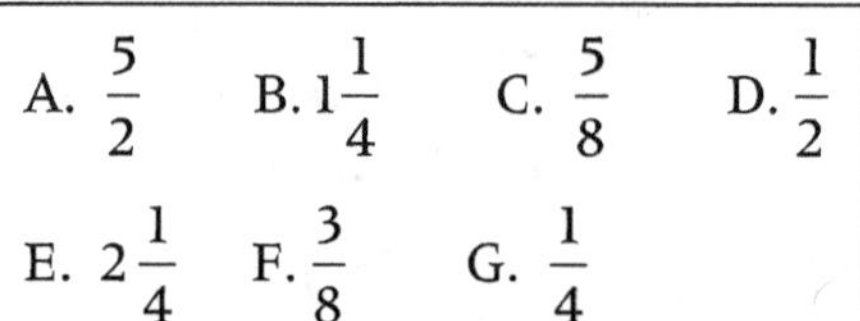 is showing three equal parts of a whole.

2. The fraction of shaded part in  is greater than the fraction of shaded part in a triangle.

3. $\dfrac{7}{7}$ represents one 7th part of the whole.

	1	3	4		1	2	3
(a)	T	T	F	(b)	F	T	F
(c)	F	T	T	(d)	T	F	F

12. Fill in the blanks.

> A. $\dfrac{5}{2}$ B. $1\dfrac{1}{4}$ C. $\dfrac{5}{8}$ D. $\dfrac{1}{2}$
>
> E. $2\dfrac{1}{4}$ F. $\dfrac{3}{8}$ G. $\dfrac{1}{4}$

1. The figure ✿ represents........ shaded part.

2. In the picture .... part of the trees are encircled.

3. .... fraction of letters in the word FRACTION are vowels.

4. ⬤ = 1 whole, then ◑⊕ equals to

	1	2	3	4		1	2	3	4
(a)	G	B	A	F	(b)	C	A	D	G
(c)	A	G	C	E	(d)	C	D	F	B

13. Kristine asked her friends to make invitation cards for the farewell party. Zoya made 5 cards, Jeniffer made 1 card, Dany made 2 cards and Linda made no cards.

Match the following columns with the fraction showing the shaded part to the number of cards made by each one.

Column A		Column B
A. Zoya	1.	
B. Jeniffer	2.	
C. Dany	3.	
D. Linda	4.	

	A	B	C	D			A	B	C	D
(a)	1	2	3	4		(b)	3	2	1	4
(c)	4	3	2	1		(d)	3	1	4	2

14. Rachel's mother bought 45 pieces of handkerchieves. Rachel used two new handkerchieves everyday. The fraction of handkerchieves not used by her in 10 days.

(a) $\dfrac{25}{45}$ (b) $\dfrac{15}{45}$

(c) $\dfrac{10}{45}$ (d) $\dfrac{20}{45}$

15. Arrange the below fractions in descending order.
$$\frac{7}{4}, \frac{5}{4}, \frac{11}{4}, \frac{9}{4}$$

(a) $\dfrac{11}{4} > \dfrac{9}{4} > \dfrac{5}{4} > \dfrac{7}{4}$

(b) $\dfrac{9}{4} > \dfrac{11}{4} > \dfrac{7}{4} > \dfrac{5}{4}$

(c) $\dfrac{5}{4} > \dfrac{9}{4} > \dfrac{7}{4} > \dfrac{11}{4}$

(d) $\dfrac{11}{4} > \dfrac{9}{4} > \dfrac{7}{4} > \dfrac{5}{4}$

16. Which fraction is second greatest fraction after arranging the fractions $\dfrac{3}{12}, \dfrac{3}{7}, \dfrac{3}{9}$ and $\dfrac{3}{8}$ in ascending order?

(a) $\dfrac{3}{7}$ (b) $\dfrac{3}{12}$ (c) $\dfrac{3}{8}$ (d) $\dfrac{3}{9}$

17. Observe the operations on fractions given below:
$$\frac{7}{10} - \frac{4}{10} = \frac{A}{B}$$
$$\frac{3}{15} + \frac{8}{15} = \frac{C}{D}$$

What is the value of $(B - A) + (D - C)$?

(a) 3   (b) 11

(c) 4   (d) 10

18. Which symbol will make the given number sentence true?
$$\frac{1}{9} + \frac{4}{9} - \frac{2}{9} \ \square \ \frac{5}{9} + \frac{2}{9} - \frac{3}{9}$$

(a) >   (b) <

(c) =

(d) Cannot be determined

19. Match the following and select the correct option.

Column A		Column B	
P.	$\dfrac{5}{9} - \dfrac{4}{9}$	(i)	$\dfrac{7}{11}$
Q.	$\dfrac{2}{4} + \dfrac{1}{4} + \dfrac{3}{4}$	(ii)	$\dfrac{1}{9}$
R.	$\dfrac{2}{11} + \dfrac{9}{11} - \dfrac{4}{11}$	(iii)	$\dfrac{8}{19}$
S.	$\dfrac{14}{19} - \dfrac{6}{19}$	(iv)	$\dfrac{6}{4}$

(a) P-(i), Q-(iv), R-(iii), S-(ii)
(b) P-(ii), Q-(iv), R-(i), S-(iii)
(c) P-(ii), Q-(i), R-(iv), S-(iii)
(d) P-(iii), Q-(iv), R-(i), S-(ii)

20.

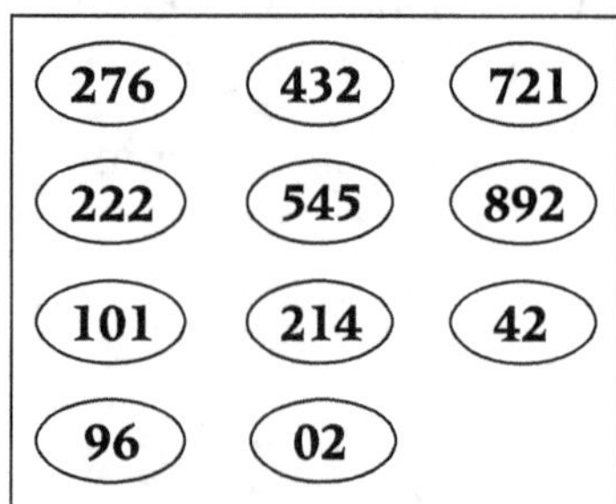

Find all such numbers which have an odd digit at the tens place in the given collection. What is the fraction of such numbers in the given collection?

(a) $\dfrac{4}{11}$ (b) $\dfrac{2}{11}$ (c) $\dfrac{6}{11}$ (d) $\dfrac{5}{11}$

Directions (Q. Nos. 21 and 22) *Deborah has 24 musical instruments. She drew a circle and divided it into parts to show the fraction of the number of musical instruments she has.*

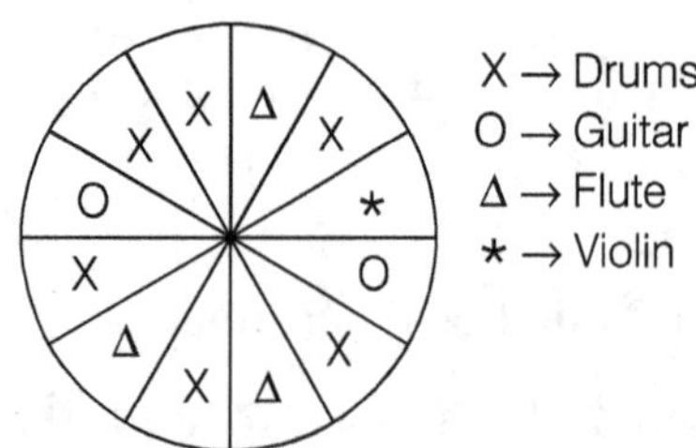

21. How many guitars does Deborah have?

(a) 2   (b) 4
(c) 6   (d) 8

22. If Deborah gives one-third of her flutes to her brother, then what is the number of flutes she left with?

(a) 6   (b) 4
(c) 2   (d) 8

23. Find the sum of shaded fractions of the given figures.

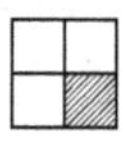 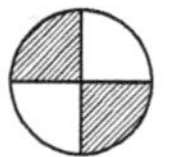 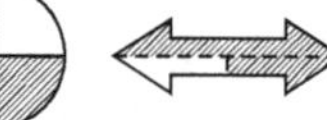

(a) $\dfrac{8}{4}$ (b) $\dfrac{5}{4}$

(c) $\dfrac{6}{4}$ (d) $\dfrac{7}{4}$

24. The Venn diagram below shows the favourite drink for 20 students.

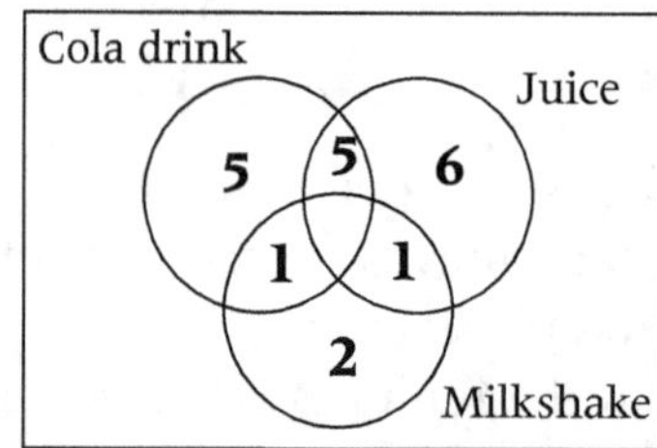

What fraction of students like juice and not milkshake?

(a) $\dfrac{5}{20}$ (b) $\dfrac{7}{20}$

(c) $\dfrac{11}{20}$ (d) $\dfrac{13}{20}$

Measurements

1. What is the height of the elephant?

(a) 28 cm   (b) 45 cm
(c) 38 cm   (d) 42 cm

2. Which of the following is longer?

(a) Pen
(b) Pencil
(c) Both are of same lengths
(d) Cannot be determined

3. John used a safety pin of length 3 cm to measure the length of his hairbrush.

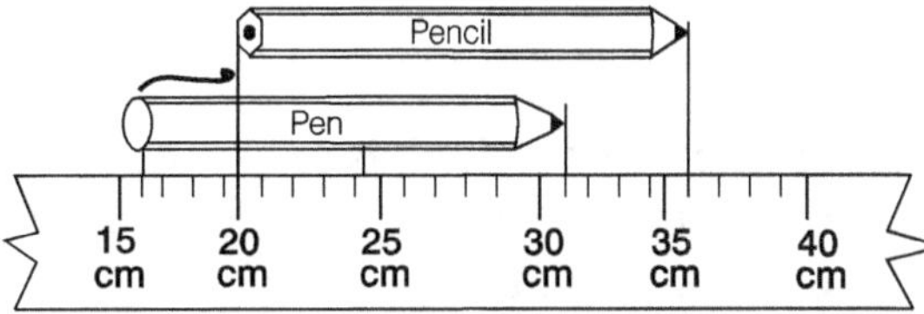

Seven such safety pins can cover the length of hairbrush. What is the length of the hairbrush?

(a) 7 cm   (b) 14 cm
(c) 21 cm   (d) 42 cm

4. Which thermometer shows 77°F?

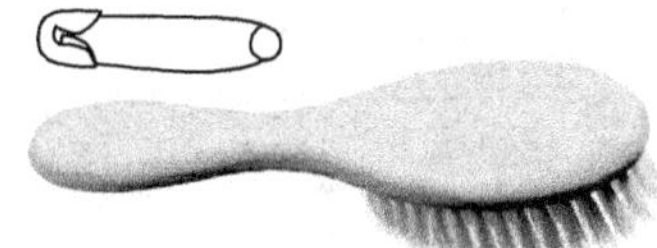

5. The temperature shown in the thermometer is 25°F more than the room temperature. Find the room temperature.

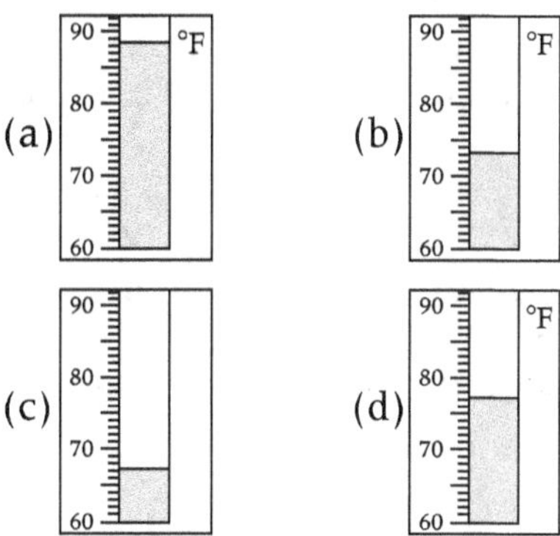

(a) 12° F   (b) 13° F
(c) 14° F   (d) 15° F

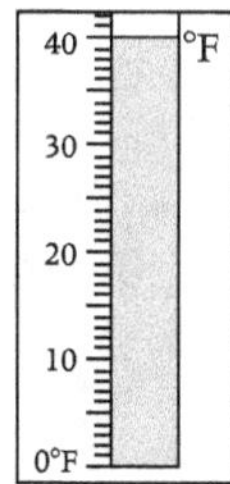

6. A road map of the surrounding places of Amia's house is shown below:

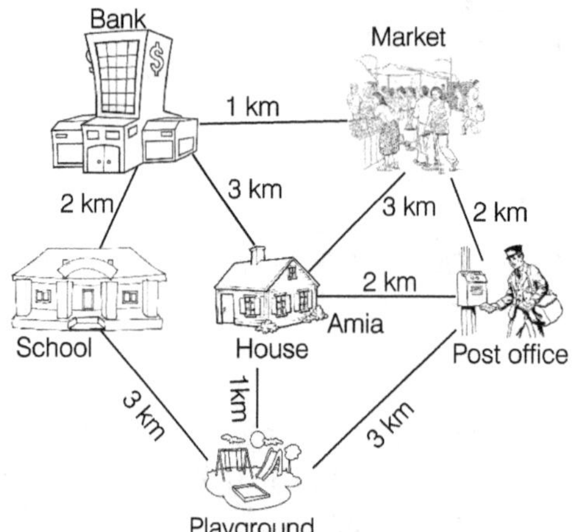

What is the shortest route from the school to Amia's house?

(a) School → Bank → Market → House

(b) School → Bank → House

(c) School → Playground → House

(d) None of the above

7. Raghav and Mehul start walk towards play ground at the same time from the points A and B respectively as shown in the figure. Point C denotes the playground.

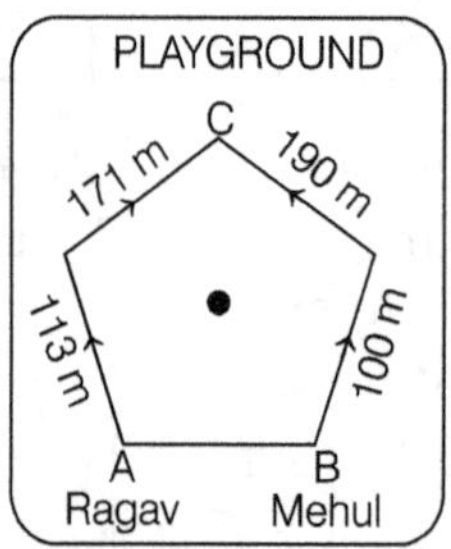

If they walk with the same speed who will reach the playground first?

(a) Raghav

(b) Mehul

(c) Both reach at the same time

(d) Cannot be determined

8. Which of the following weight scales shows the correct weight of the object?

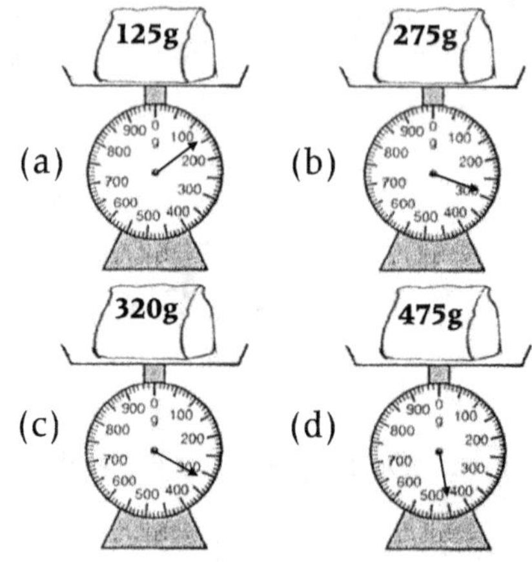

9. What is the mass of the bag of coins shown in the picture given below?

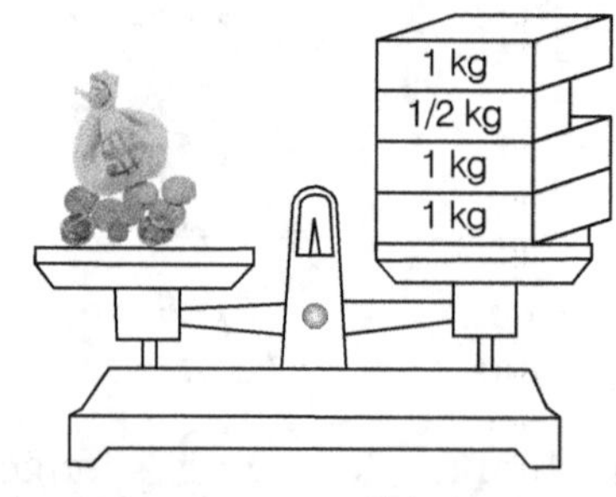

(a) 1200 g   (b) 130 g

(c) 3500 g   (d) 1.5 kg

10. A vegetable vendor has to weight 2550 g of tomatoes. Which of the following combination of weights will he use?

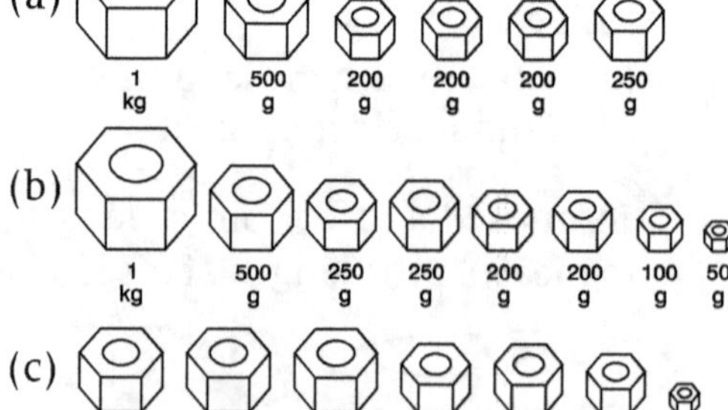

(d) None of the above

11. Linda went to two different fruit shops to buy fruits.

The diagram below shows the weights of two baskets of fruits she bought.

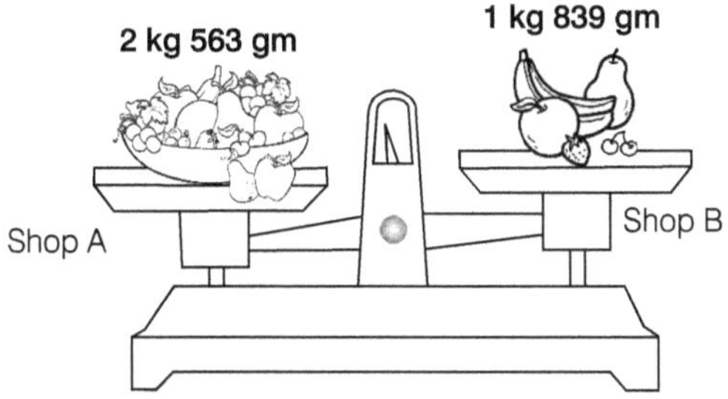

How much more fruits did she buy from shop A?

(a) 4 kg 402 g

(b) 724 g

(c) 1 kg 724 g

(d) 1000 g

12. Jeniffer is 5 kg lighter than Shelly. Maria is 12 kg heavier than Shelly. If Shelly is 25 kg, then what is the total weight of Shelly, Jeniffer and Maria?

(a) 102 kg   (b) 82 kg

(c) 85 kg   (d) 92 kg

13. Sonam made a mocktail using three different types of juices. She poured 725 ml of orange juice, 845 ml of pineapple juice and 965 ml of cranberry juice in a jug. What is the quantity of juice made by her?

(a) 2 L 535 ml

(b) 23 L 53 ml

(c) 253 ml

(d) 2 L 53 ml

14. A bucket can hold 2 L of water. It is being filled with water by the mugs of different capacity. What combination of mugs can fill the bucket?

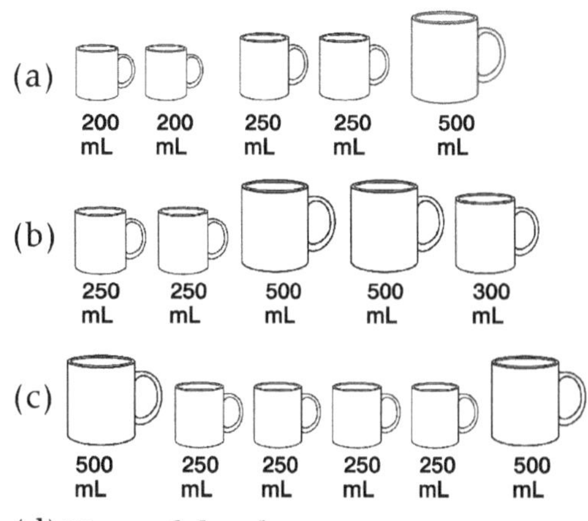

(d) None of the above

15. Richard had 6  each of capacity 3L 35 ml. If one of the pack fell on the floor, then how much quantity of milk is left with him?

(a) 18 L 750 ml

(b) 20 L 100 ml

(c) 16 L 750 ml

(d) 15 L 175 ml

16. Misthi bought a big-can of 7 L of Gemini oil. She used a 700 ml beaker to keep the oil for daily use. How many times can this beaker be refilled by the oil from the can?

(a) 100

(b) 20

(c) 10

(d) 70

17. A jug of capacity 2 L can be half filled by pouring 5 full mugs of water into it.

How much water does the mug hold when it is, half?

(a) 200 ml   (b) 150 ml

(c) 250 ml   (d) 100 ml

18. Distance between the bank and the mall is twice the distance between John's home and mall. Find the distance travelled by John.

(a) From his home to bank and back home.

(b) From mall to bank and back to his home.

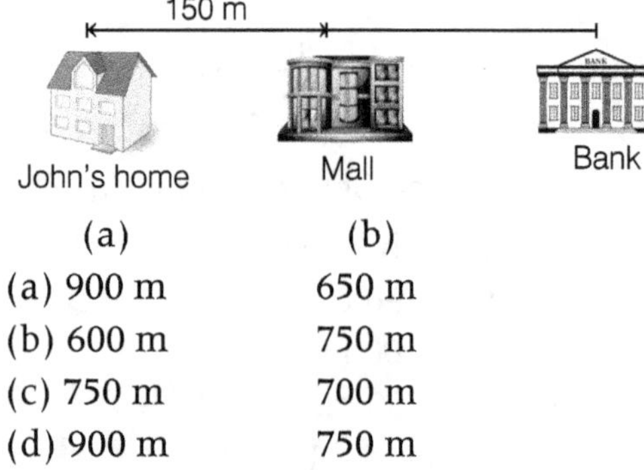

      (a)   (b)

(a) 900 m   650 m

(b) 600 m   750 m

(c) 750 m   700 m

(d) 900 m   750 m

19. The weight of one △ is 250 g.

What is the weight of one ☐?

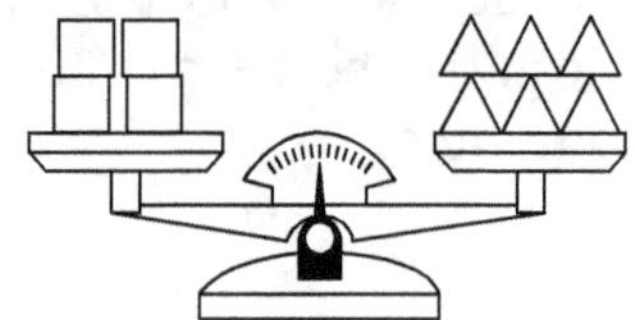

(a) 375 g   (b) 500 g

(c) 390 g   (d) 425 g

20. Fill in the blanks.

A. 1862	B. 7	C. 400
D. 1342	E. 700	F. 38
G. 150	H. 46	I. 10

1. Shelly bought 266 cm of ribbon and cut it into seven equal parts, ... cm is the length of each part.

2. Greg bought 746 g of sugar and used 596 g of it. .... g of sugar is left with him.

3. Rondish mixed 250 ml of lemon juice and 450 ml of water to make lemonade. .... ml of lemonade is made by him.

4. Shenaya bought 1046 g of potatoes and 5954 g of onions. She bought a total of .... kg of vegetables.

Codes

	1	2	3	4
(a)	G	B	C	D
(b)	F	G	E	B
(c)	A	C	F	I
(d)	None of the above			

Money

1. Michelle has ₹ 452 in her piggy bank. The amount she has in paise is
   (a) 45.2 paise
   (b) 4520 paise
   (c) 45200 paise
   (d) 452 paise

2. Braden has five hundred forty six rupees fifty paise in his pocket. Which of the following fruits can he buy from the money?

1 kg Apples ₹ 527.40	1 kg Mangoes ₹ 572.00	1 kg Guava ₹ 556.75

   (a) Apple
   (b) Mango
   (c) Guava
   (d) None of these

3. After buying a pair of shoes for ₹ 1500, Sandy had thirty five thousand paise left. What amount of money Sandy had before?
   (a) ₹ 1500 + ₹ 350
   (b) ₹ 1500 × ₹ 350
   (c) ₹ 1500 − ₹ 350
   (d) ₹ 1500 ÷ ₹ 350

4. In how many ways can ₹6.25 be obtained from the following coins?

   (a) 6   (b) 5   (c) 4   (d) 3

5. Anjali has 12 rupees 60 paise to buy a notebook. The cost of notebook is 9 rupees 50 paise. How much change should she get back?
   (a) 3100 paise
   (b) ₹ 31
   (c) 310 paise
   (d) ₹ 310

6. Tyran had ₹ 400.25. He paid ₹ 180.75 for a ticket to a football match. At the match, he bought a sandwich for ₹ 40.50 and a soft drink for ₹ 25.00. What amount of money is left with him?
   (a) ₹ 150.75
   (b) ₹ 165.25
   (c) ₹ 150
   (d) ₹ 154

Directions (Q.Nos. 7 and 8) Zara and her brother Zack go to the gift shop at the mall with their parents. The table below shows the prices of the items at the gift shop.

Gift shop price list

Items	Price
Toy bike	₹ 210.25
Toy submarine	₹ 375.50
Dancing doll	₹ 308.75
Sea animal sticker	₹ 175

7. Zara could only buy items worth ₹ 350. What can she buy from the list?

(a) Toy bike and toy submarine

(b) Only dancing doll

(c) Sea animal sticker and toy bike

(d) Only toy submarine

8. Zack firstly bought toy submarine, then he got it exchanged for toy bike. How much money will he get back?

(a) ₹ 165.25   (b) ₹ 375.50

(c) ₹ 150.25   (d) None of these

9. Match the following

List-I	List-II
A. ₹ 5.50 + 25 paisa	1. ₹ 5.25
B. ₹ 5.75 − 50 paisa	2. ₹ 5.75
C. ₹ 5.25 + 75 paisa	3. ₹ 6
D. ₹ 5.75 + 10 paisa	4. ₹ 5.80
E. ₹ 5.90 − 10 paisa	5. ₹ 5.85

     A   B   C   D   E

(a) 2   1   3   4   5

(b) 3   1   2   5   4

(c) 3   4   2   5   1

(d) 2   1   3   5   4

10. Rohit spent the amount of money shown below:

If Rohit had ₹ 2000 in the beginning, then how much amount of money is left with him?

(a) ₹ 1306   (b) ₹ 1351

(c) ₹ 1341   (d) ₹ 1441

Directions (Q.Nos. 11 and 12) Consider the following picture to answer questions.

11. The total amount of money shown in the figure is ………. .

(a) ₹ 182   (b) ₹ 185   (c) ₹ 187   (d) ₹ 177

12. If the total money is to be divided equally among 5 boys, how much each boy will get?

(a) ₹ 39.50   (b) ₹ 36.40

(c) ₹ 35   (d) ₹ 37.40

13. Sheen bought six stickers for 35 paise each. How much did they cost her?

(a) 2 rupees 35 paise

(b) 2 rupees 10 paise

(c) 3 rupees 5 paise

(d) None of the above

14. State 'T' for true or 'F' for false.

1. The Indian unit of money is rupee.

2. Symbol for paise is ₹.

3. 1000 paise makes 1 rupee.

4. If cost of one stamp is 15 paise, then cost of 40 stamps is ₹ 6.

     1   2   3   4

(a) T   T   T   F

(b) F   F   T   T

(c) T   F   F   T

(d) F   F   T   F

15. Fill in the blanks.

A. ₹ 175	B. ₹ 1.75
C. ₹ 1.70	D. 15 paise
E. 50 paise	F. 75 paise
G. ₹ 2.70	

1. If two coins, each of 10 paise, 25 paise and 50 paise is added to ₹ 1, then the total amount of money will be ....

2. If the sum of money presented in the rectangle is ₹ 1, then .... comes in place of question mark.

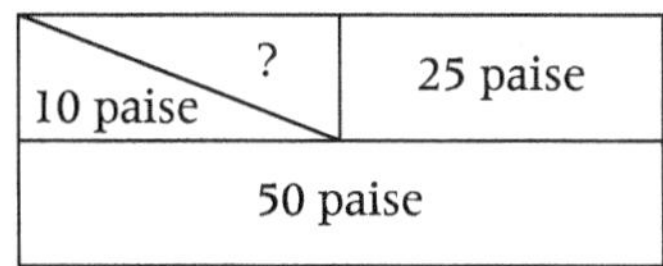

3. 1 rupee 75 paise is same as ....

4. Five 10 paise coins is equal to ....

	1	2	3	4
(a)	B	E	A	D
(b)	G	D	B	E
(c)	C	F	B	D
(d)	None of the above

16. John earns ₹ 560 a month. He spends ₹ 440 every month. How much money does he save in a year?
(a) ₹ 1680
(b) ₹ 1270
(c) ₹ 2940
(d) ₹ 1440

17. A school teacher and 16 students went to a museum. The price chart of tickets is given below:

Tickets	Rates
Adult	Forty six rupees and seventy five paise
Child	Nineteen rupees and seventy five paise

What is the total cost of the tickets?
(a) ₹ 36.75
(b) ₹ 300.75
(c) ₹ 36.275
(d) ₹ 362.75

18. If
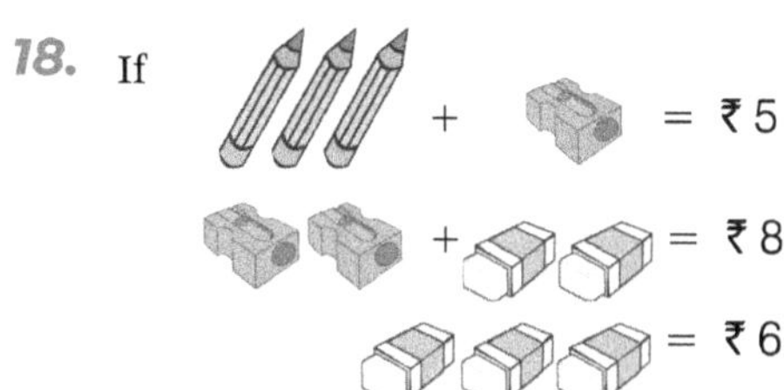
Then, the cost of one pencil is
(a) ₹ 1   (b) ₹ 2
(c) ₹ 3   (d) ₹ 5

19. A video game costs ₹750. Jack save 2500 paise every week. How many weeks must he save to buy the video game?
(a) 25   (b) 30
(c) 32   (d) 40

20. George went to a mall for shopping with ₹ 1200 and saw the following offers.

Which of the following offer he can take so that no amount will left with him.
(a) A bag and a jeans
(b) A watch and a T-shirt
(c) A jeans and a T-shirt
(d) A bag and a watch

21. Jinnie has ₹ 133 in her piggy bank. Her grandparents give him ₹ 16 to add to her bank. After that, every week, Jinnie adds 12 rupees 50 paise to her piggy bank. How much money does she have in her piggy bank after 6 weeks?

(a) ₹ 2 hundred 2 tens 4 ones

(b) ₹ 22 hundred 4 ones

(c) ₹ 2 tens 4 ones

(d) None of the above

22. Mr. Crust Cafe's bills are given below:

Mr. Crust Cafe	
Breakfast on the go	
* * * * * * * * *	
1 fruit pastry	₹ 20.75
1 cappuccino	₹ 35.50
1 cafe blast	₹ 50.25

A

Mr. Crust Cafe	
Breakfast on the go	
* * * * * * * * *	
1 trufle cake	₹ 20.25
1 soft drink	₹ 30.75
1 mango cupcake	₹ 15.00

B

Mr. Crust Cafe	
Breakfast on the go	
* * * * * * * * *	
2 paneer wrap	₹ 40.45
1 pancake	₹ 13.15
3 coffees	₹ 75.00

C

Mr. Crust Cafe	
Breakfast on the go	
* * * * * * * * *	
5 donuts	₹ 60.50
3 waffle strips	₹ 30.00
4 milkshake	₹ 20.50

D

Which bill has the highest amount?

(a) B   (b) C

(c) A   (d) D

23. Carol and John go to a stationary store to buy pencils and pens. One pack of pencils costs 10 rupees 50 paise and 1 pack of pens costs 15 rupees 25 paise. Carol bought 1 pack of pencils and 4 packs of pens. John bought 2 packs of pencils and 2 packs of pens.

How much more money does Carol spend than John?

(a) ₹ 30.5   (b) ₹ 121.5

(c) ₹ 20   (d) ₹ 30

24. A shop has the following offer.

Gabriella wants to buy 10 shirts for her brother. If one shirt cost ₹ 200, then how much money she has to pay after discount?

(a) ₹ 500   (b) ₹ 1000

(c) ₹ 1500   (d) ₹ 2000

Time and Calendar

1. The principal of a school announced to hold the morning prayer exactly after 15 minutes. The current time in the morning is shown below in the clock.

   At what time will the prayer start?
   (a) 8 : 30 am   (b) 8 : 00 am
   (c) 9 : 15 am   (d) 8 : 18 am

2. What time will be shown by the missing clock?

  **?** 

   (a) 3 : 30   (b) 4 : 30
   (c) 4 : 25   (d) 3 : 25

3. Luisy started cooking a cake at the time shown below:

   It needs to be cooked for 150 minutes. At what time will the cake be ready?
   (a) 3 : 50   (b) 3 : 45
   (c) 3 : 55   (d) 3 : 30

4. Mandy woke up in the morning and saw the clock. The minute hand of the clock was on 7 and the hour hand was between 7 and 8. What was the time when Mandy woke up?
   (a) 8 : 07 am   (b) 8 : 35 am
   (c) 7 : 07 am   (d) 7 : 35 am

5. The metro train schedule has some missing times. The same amount of time passes between each train.

Train Times	5 : 05	5 : 20	5 : 35	?	6 : 05

   What is the missing time in the table?
   (a) 5 h 20 min   (b) 6 h
   (c) 5 h 50 min   (d) 5 h 45 min

6. Linda left home at 11 : 00 am. She spent 15 min walking to Staley's house and then stayed there for 2 h 15 min. Linda, then spent another 15 min to come back to home. At what time did Linda arrive home?
   (a) Quarter to 1   (b) Quarter to 2
   (c) Quarter past 1   (d) Quarter past 12

7. Robins arranged to meet Lisa at the shopping mall at 4 : 45 pm. Lisa is half an hour late. If Robins reached the mall at 15 min earlier. How many minutes had he waited for Lisa?
   (a) 35 min   (b) 45 min
   (c) 30 min   (d) 55 min

7. Robins arranged to meet Lisa at the shopping mall at 4 : 45 pm. Lisa is half an hour late. If Robins reached the mall at 15 min earlier. How many minutes had he waited for Lisa?
(a) 35 min   (b) 45 min
(c) 30 min   (d) 55 min

8. Which of the following is equivalent to 67 days?
(a) 6 weeks 4 days
(b) 8 weeks 1 day
(c) 9 weeks 4 days
(d) 12 weeks 5 days

9. Robin's sister is 8 weeks old. His friend's sister is 6 weeks 10 days old. How many more days old is Robin's sister than his friend's sister?
(a) 1 week   (b) 5 days
(c) 4 days   (d) Half week

10. Fill in the blanks.

A. 28	B. Friday
C. 14 days	D. 21 days
E. Saturday	F. Thursday

1. Number of days in 3 weeks is ....
2. Five days before Wednesday is ....
3. .... days make a month of February in an ordinary year.
4. If 3 days later is Tuesday, then today is ....

Codes

	1	2	3	4		1	2	3	4
(a)	A	B	D	C	(b)	C	E	A	B
(c)	A	F	C	B	(d)	D	B	A	E

11. Jane will come back from his school trip in exactly two days. How many hours is it until he returns?
(a) 20 h   (b) 24 h
(c) 48 h   (d) 60 h

12. Use the calendar given in the picture and answer the following question.

August 2015						
Sun	Mon	Tue	Wed	Thu	Fri	Sat
						1
2	3	4	5	6	7	8
9	10	11	12	13	14	15
16	17	18	19	20	21	22
23	24	25	26	27	28	29
30	31					

Ralph and Sammi planned to meet every Saturday. If today's date is 8th August, then how many number of Saturdays will they meet after today?
(a) 2   (b) 3
(c) 4   (d) 1

13. If Niharika takes a leave on 2nd Thursday and 4th Saturday in August 2020, then how many days are working? (Assume that every Sunday and Independence day is a holiday).

August 2020						
Sun	Mon	Tue	Wed	Thu	Fri	Sat
		1	2	3	4	5	6
7	8	9	10	11	12	13
14	15	16	17	18	19	20
21	22	23	24	25	26	27
28	29	30	31			

(a) 24   (b) 23
(c) 25   (d) 26

14. A Gorilla grows 3m each week. A dinosaur grows 1 m each day. In 3 week how much does a dinosaur grow than a Gorilla?
(a) 25m   (b) 28m
(c) 41m   (d) 12m

15. State whether 'T' for true or 'F' for false.

1. The short hand of the clock is called the minute hand.
2. The hour hand takes 12 h to complete one round.
3. There are 300 sec in 30 min.
4. 6 months in an year have 31 days.

Codes

	1	2	3	4
(a)	F	T	F	F
(b)	T	T	F	F
(c)	T	F	F	F
(d)	F	F	T	F

16. Sheeba's sister was born on 29th February, 2000. If it is 2013 now, after how many years can she celebrate her sister's birthday?

(a) 2 yr (b) 3 yr
(c) 1 yr (d) 4 yr

Directions (Q.Nos. 17-18) Read the following information carefully.

Class III students are going to visit Delhi on a field trip. During the field trip they are going to visit three different locations. Using the chart below, answer the questions.

Attraction	Arrive	Leave
Jawahar Lal Nehru Stadium	8 : 30 am	10 : 20 am
Nehru Planetarium	12 : 15 pm	
Red Fort		7 : 00 pm

17. For how long did the class stay at Jawahar Lal Nehru Stadium?

(a) 50 min (b) 1 h 40 min
(c) 2 h (d) 1 h 50 min

18. The students stayed for 2 hours 15 minutes in Nehru Planetarium. At what time did they leave?

(a) 2 : 30 pm
(b) 2 : 15 pm
(c) 1 : 45 pm
(d) None of the above

19. Mishi has to catch a train to Sweden. Trains arrive after every 40 minutes. If the first train arrives at 7 : 10 am, then the fourth train will arrive at

(a) 8 : 30 am (b) 9 : 10 am
(c) 10 : 15 am (d) 10 : 10 am

20. June 16th is circled on the calendar below:

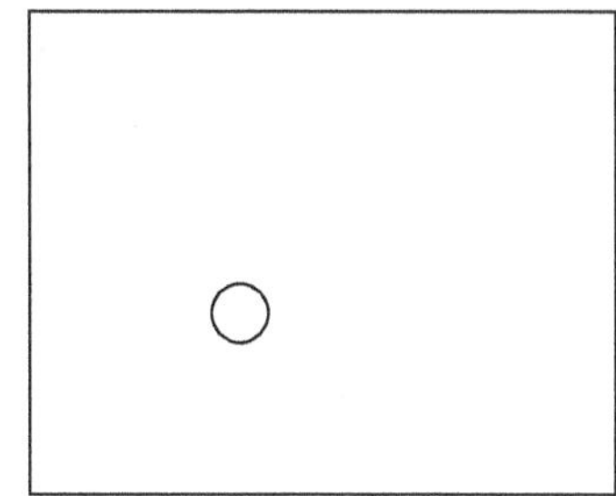

S	M	T	W	T	F	S
			1	2	3	4
5	6	7	8	9	10	11
12	13	14	15	16	17	18
19	20	21	22	23	24	25
26	27	28	29	30	31	

What will be the date after 3 weeks and 3 days from June 16th?

(a) 9th July
(b) 8th July
(c) 12th July
(d) 10th July

Chapter

08

Shapes

1. Which of the following have a curve edge?

(a) Pen (b) Car
(c) Coin (d) Pencil box

2. Which figure is different from others?

(a) 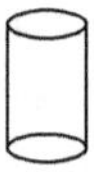 (b) 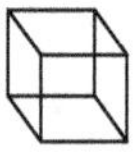 (c) 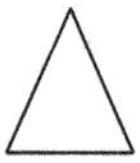 (d) 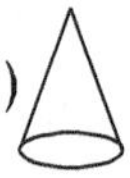

3. Which one of the following is the best example of a cone?

(a) 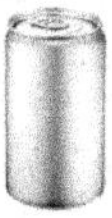 (b) 

(c) 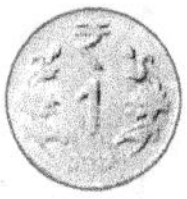 (d) 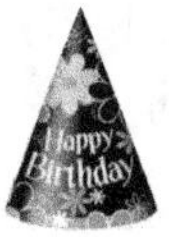

4. Raman wants to draw a circle with the help of the given objects.

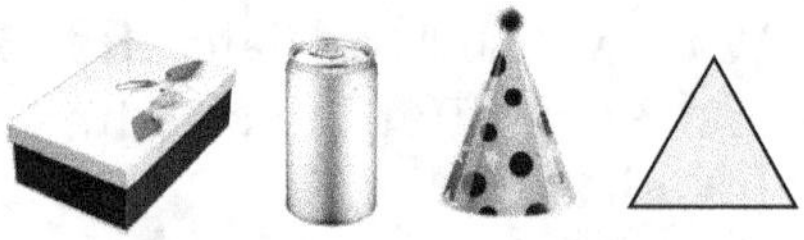

P Q R S

Which of the following objects can he use?

(a) Only S (b) Both P and Q
(c) Only R (d) Both Q and R

5. How many line segments is used to make given figure?

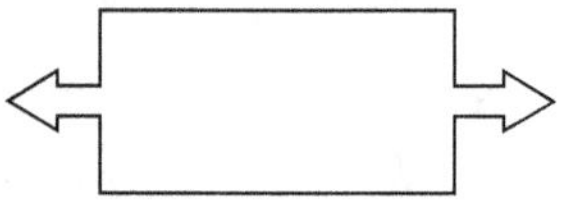

(a) 20
(b) 15
(c) 12
(d) 18

6. Match the following List-I to List-II :

List-I	List-II
A. 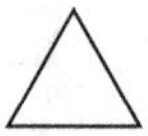	1. 6 line segments
B. 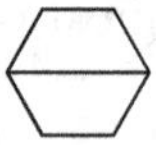	2. 3 line segments
C. 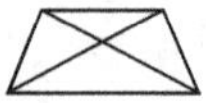	3. 5 line segments
D. 	4. 7 line segments

Codes

	A	B	C	D
(a)	4	1	3	2
(b)	2	4	1	3
(c)	1	2	3	4
(d)	1	4	3	2

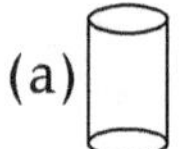

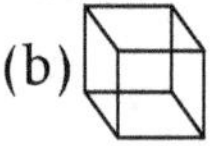

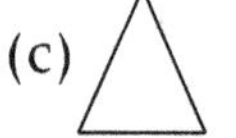

7. Ms. Jacob asked her students to draw a picture having 4 squares and 2 circles in it.

Who drew the correct figure?

(a) George   (b) Kim
(c) Micheal   (d) Karen

8. Mark draws the picture below using 2-D shapes.

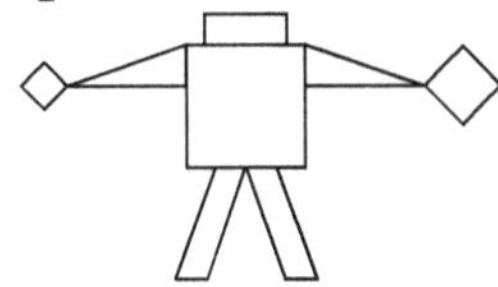

Which shapes are equal sized in his picture?

(a) Triangles
(b) Rectangles
(c) Squares
(d) Rhombuses

9. Which of the following shapes has exactly 3 faces and 2 curved edges.

(a) 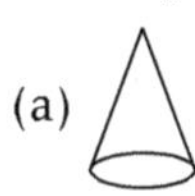   (c) 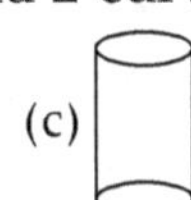

(b) 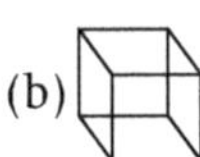   (d) 

10. How many number of corners does 4 squares and 3 triangles have

(a) 25   (b) 20
(c) 24   (d) 27

11. Monty has 15 coins of ten rupees. He put them exactly one on the others. Which shape is formed by him in such an arrangement?

(a) Cube   (b) Cond
(c) Cylinder   (d) Rectangle

12. A squirrel has walked around a given triangle completely. Find the distance covered by squirrel?

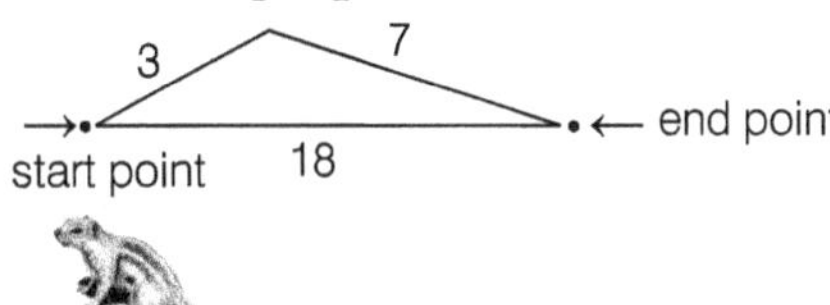

(a) 10   (b) 25
(c) 21   (d) 28

13. Jack made the following sign board on topic 'No parking'. Find the sum of length of boundary of board?

(a) 44   (b) 34
(c) 42   (d) 48

14. Match with the correct option :

A. 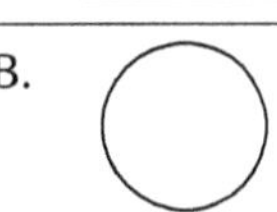	1. 3 sides and three corners
B. 	2. All sides are equal
C. 	3. Only opposite sides are equal
D.	4. No side and no corner

Codes

	A	B	C	D		A	B	C	D
(a)	4	3	2	1	(b)	3	4	2	1
(c)	1	3	2	4	(d)	2	4	1	3

15. Fill in the blanks.

A. 4	B. 1	C. 8	D. 10
E. 12	F. 3	G. 13	

1. A cuboid has.........number of edges.
2. A cylinder has..........number of faces.
3. A cone has.........number of vertices.
4. A cube has.........number of vertices.

Codes

	1	2	3	4		1	2	3	4
(a)	F	E	A	B	(b)	D	G	A	C
(c)	E	F	B	C	(d)	G	D	C	A

16. State whether 'T' for true or 'F' for false.

1. A cuboid has 2 curved edges.
2. A cube has 10 edges.
3. A cone has 3 faces.
4. A cylinder has no edges.

Codes

	1	2	3	4		1	2	3	4
(a)	F	F	F	F	(b)	F	T	T	F
(c)	T	T	T	T	(d)	T	T	T	T

17. The shape is made up of different shapes.

* It has 4 semi-circles

* It has 1 square

Which shape it is

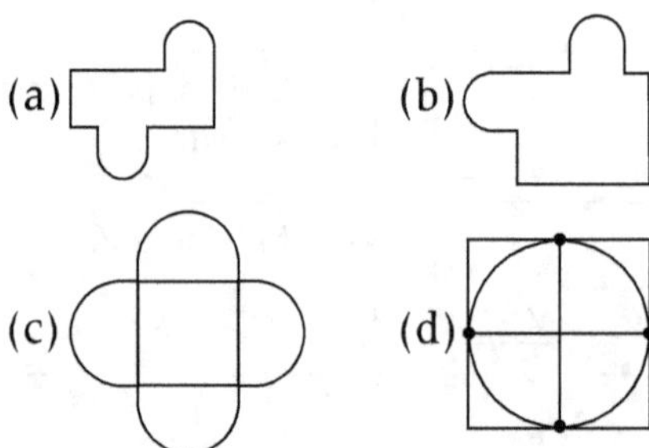

(a) (b) (c) (d)

18. A football ground is in the shape of a square. The sum of the sides of the field is 72 m. Find the sum of length of two sides of the field.

(a) 24 m   (b) 18 m
(c) 42 m   (d) 36 m

19. Ria made a pen stand for her brother. She coloured its faces with different coloured pens.

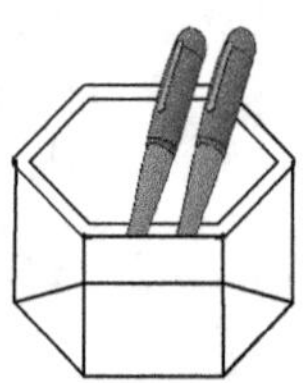

How many different coloured pen she must have used to colour the above pen stand?

(a) 5   (b) 6
(c) 7   (d) 8

20. • My name is X. I have 8 vertices and 12 edges. My opposite sides are equal.

• My name is Y. I also have 8 vertices and 12 edges like X but my all side are equal.

• My name is Z. I have 3 faces, 2 curved edges but have no vertices.

Can you find the X, Y, Z from above clues?

	X	Y	Z
(a)	Cuboid	Cone	Cube
(b)	Cylinder	Cube	Cuboid
(c)	Cube	Cuboid	Cone
(d)	Cuboid	Cube	Cylinder

Patterns and Symmetry

1. Ruchel saw different shapes arranged in a pattern as shown below:

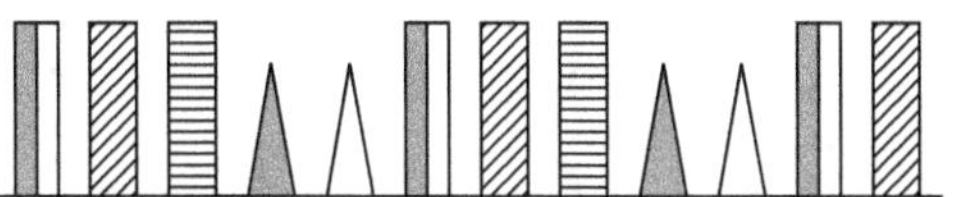

What would be the next three shapes arranged in this pattern?

(a) 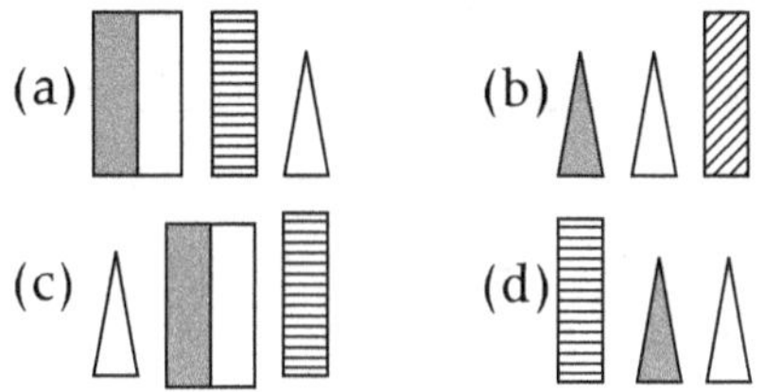

(b)

(c)

(d)

2. Look at the pattern and find the next term of the pattern.

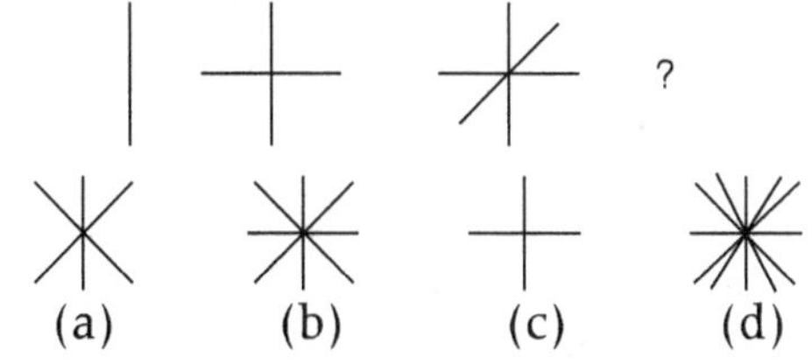

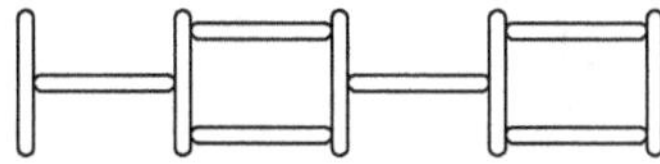

   (a)   (b)   (c)   (d)

3. Rogere is making a pattern using ice-cream sticks as shown below:

What should be the next part of the pattern?

(a)   (b)

(c)   (d)

4. Look at the pattern given below:

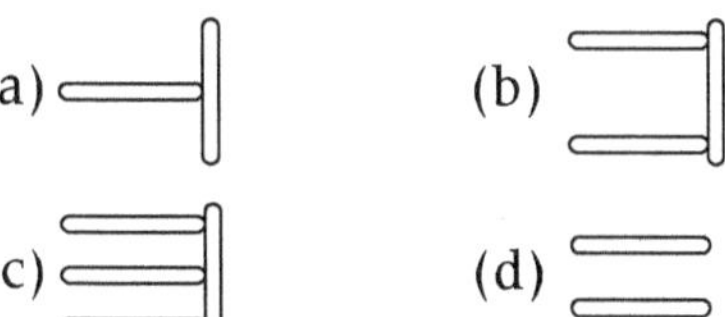

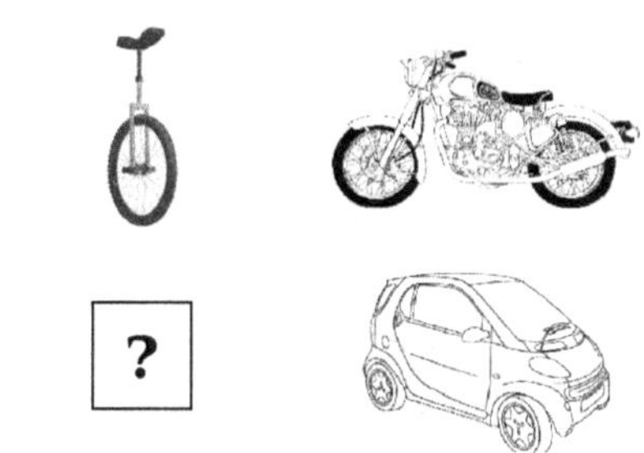

What is the missing term in the pattern?

(a) 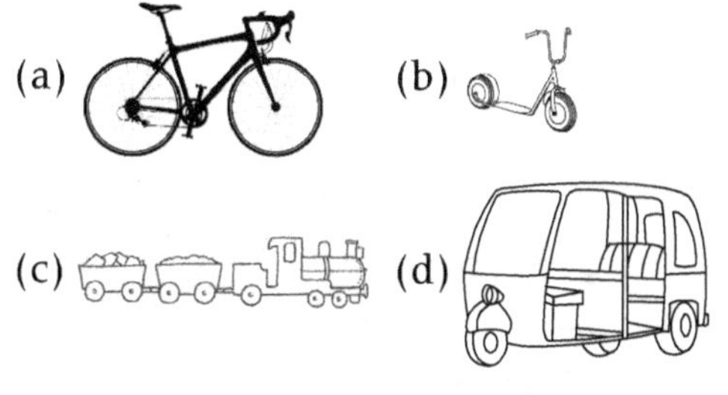   (b)

(c)   (d)

5. Grini makes a pattern around the edge of her diary.

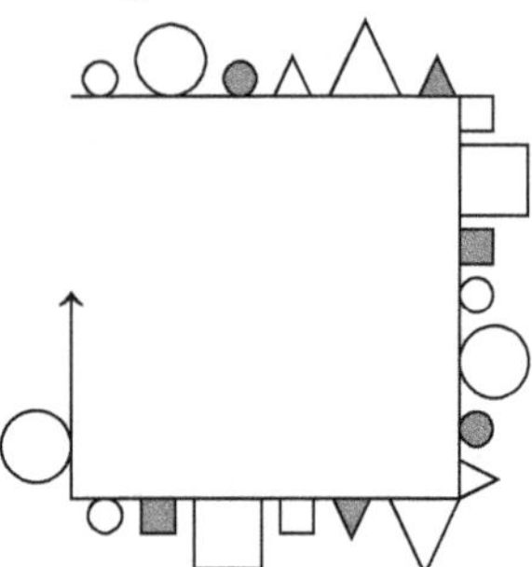

What will be the next four terms of the pattern?

(a) 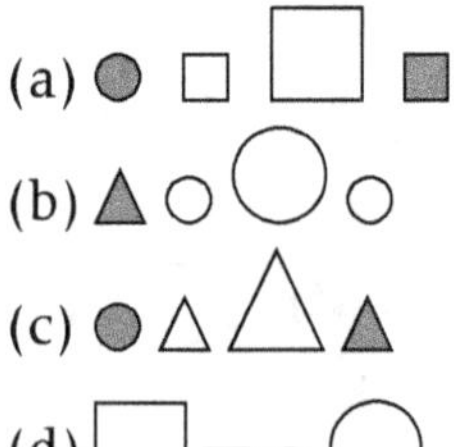

(b) ▲ ○ ○ ○

(c) ● △ △ ▲

(d) □ ▢ ● ○

6. Ronit had painted a door mat of her room using fabric colours.

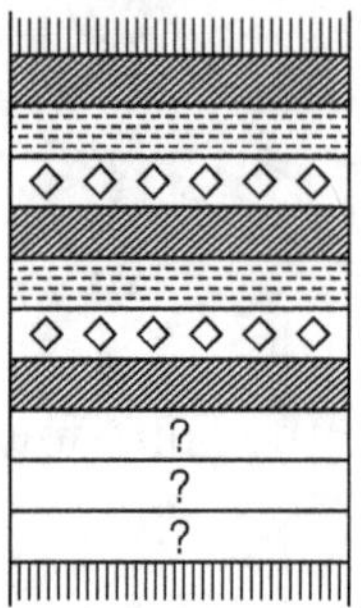

What would be the last three designs she will paint on the mat?

(a)    (b) 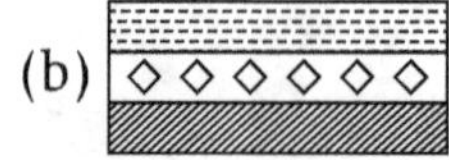

(c) 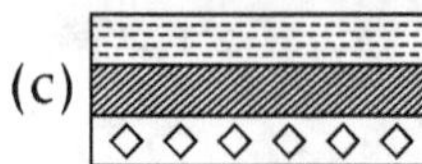   (d) None of these

7. Tina is making an art project with some buttons which follows a certain pattern find the missing button.

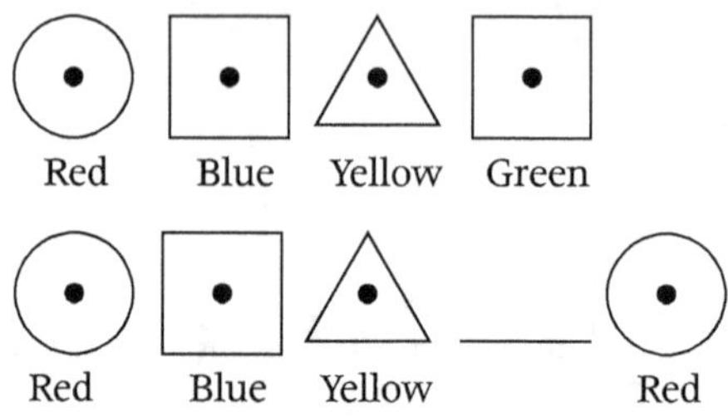

(a) A blue square
(b) A green triangle
(c) A yellow triangle
(d) A green square

8. Look at the pattern given below:

Which of the following pattern follows the same rule?

(a) 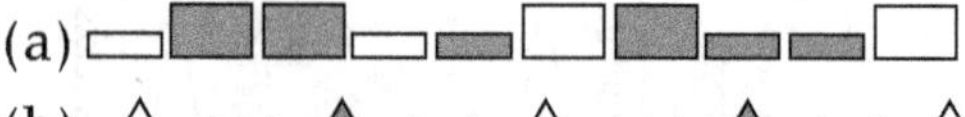

(b) 

(c) 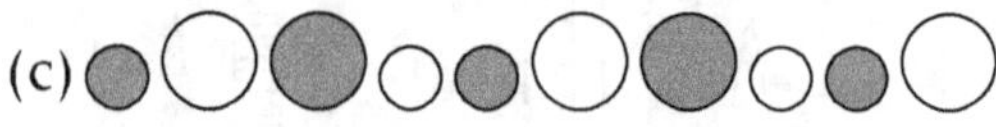

(d) None of the above

9. Dakshan is making a border for his bedroom wall as shown below. He made a mistake in the pattern followed by the border.

Which block made by him is in a wrong way?

(a) Only 1
(b) Only 2
(c) Only 3
(d) Only 4

10. Look at the pattern given below

Which option is following the same rule?

(a) 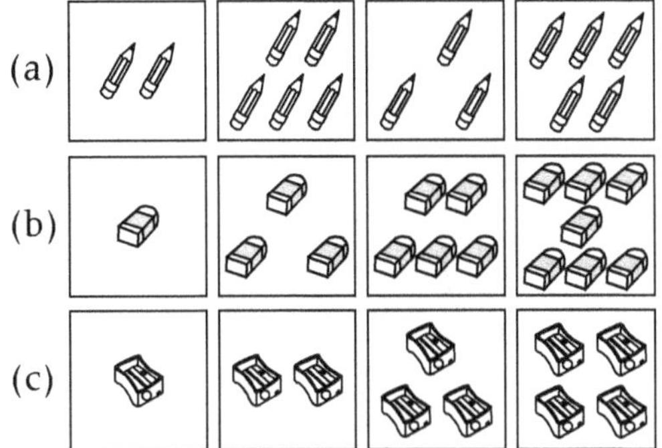

(b) 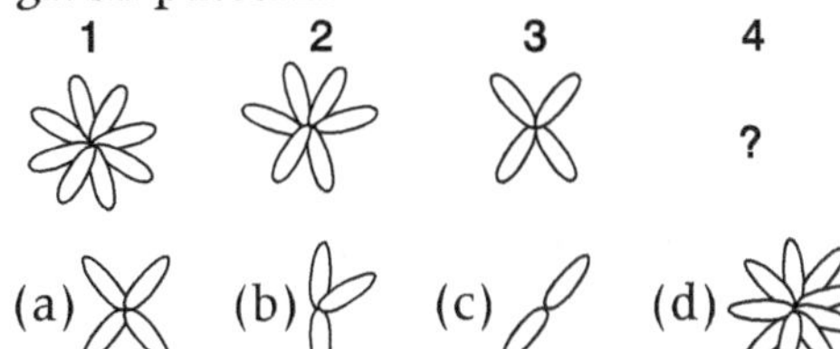

(c) 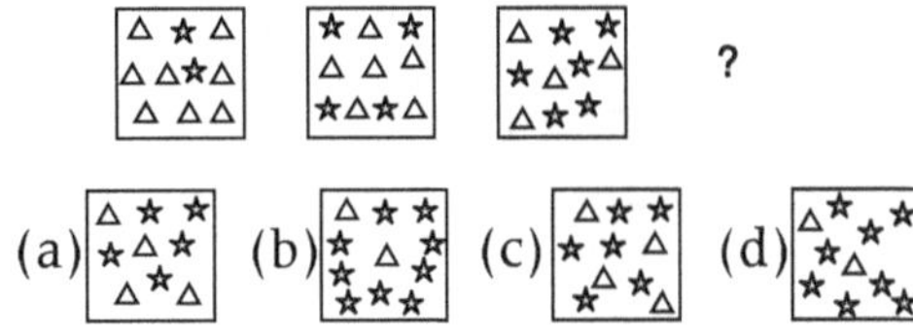

(d) None of the above

11. Which shape will be the next in the given pattern?

1   2   3   4

(a) (b) (c) (d)

12. Which figure will come next in the given pattern?

(a) (b) (c) (d)

13. A pattern of shapes is following a rule as shown below:

Which of the following would be true?
(a) The 6th term will have 15 triangles.
(b) The 6th term will have 24 triangles.

(c) The 6th term will have 18 triangles.
(d) The 6th term will have 12 triangles.

14. Tania counted the number of dots in different ladybugs.

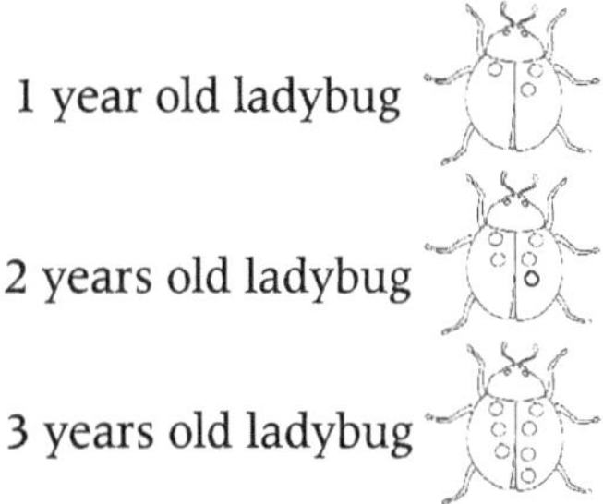

1 year old ladybug

2 years old ladybug

3 years old ladybug

How many dots will a 4 years old ladybug have?
(a) 4   (b) 6   (c) 7   (d) 9

15. Cameron makes the following number pattern using a rule.

5, 9, 13, 17, 21, 25, 29

She asked her brother to follow the rule and form another pattern. What pattern his brother should form?
(a) 7, 11, 15, 19, 23, 27, ...
(b) 6, 10, 14, 18, 22, 26, ...
(c) 13, 17, 21, 25, 29, ...
(d) All of the above

16. What will be the next two terms?

18, 16, 14, 12, ?, ?
(a) 8, 10   (b) 10, 12
(c) 12, 8   (d) 10, 8

17. Which one of the following option is correct to complete the series?

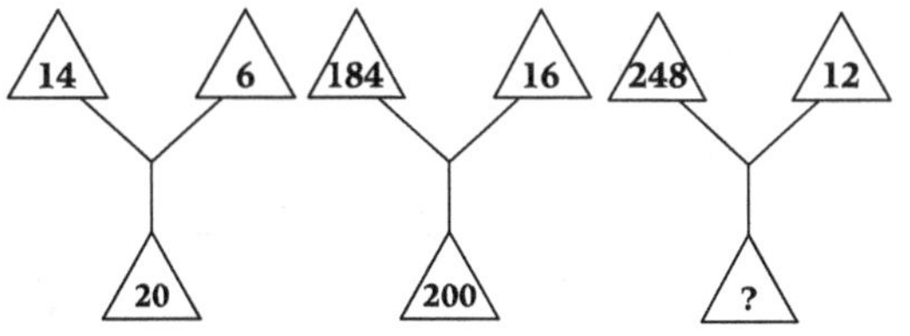

(a) 260   (b) 250
(c) 255   (d) None of these

18. Sheen was standing in her balcony on 4th floor. She saw a car parked below on the road. What view of car she must had seen?

(a)　　　　　　(b)

(c)　　　　　　(d)

19. Which of the following is symmetrical about the dashed line?

 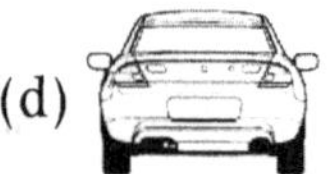

(a) --A--　　　　(b) B

(c) C　　　　　　(d) --D---

20. Which of the following is not symmetrical about the dashed line?

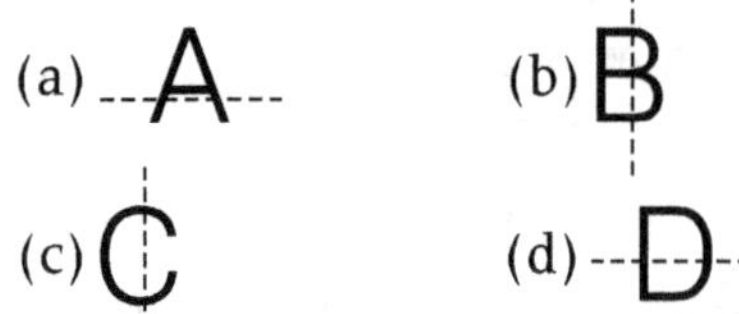

(a)　　(b)　　(c)　　(d)

21. Choose the odd one out.

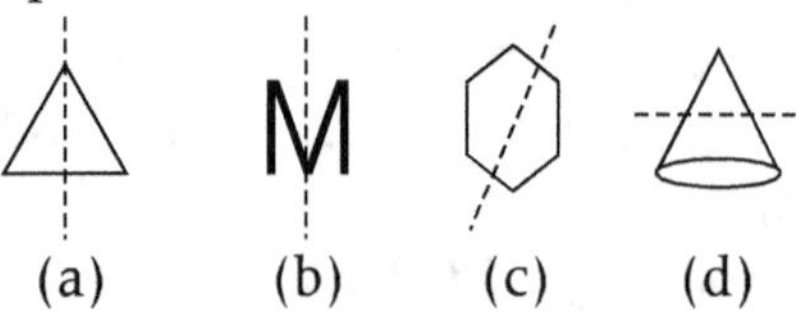

(a)　　　　　　(b)

(c)　　　　　　(d)

22. What will be next figure in the following pattern?

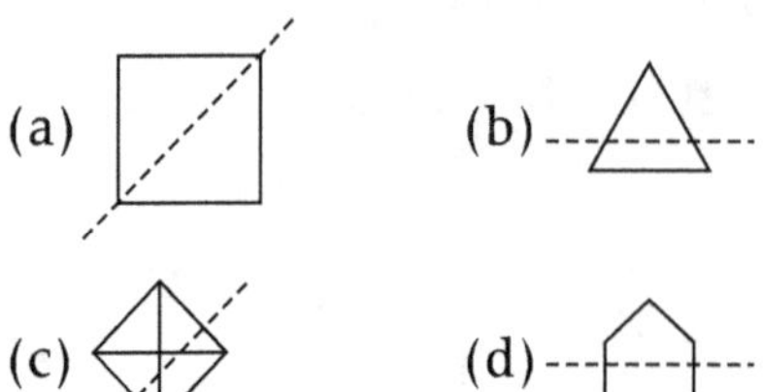

?

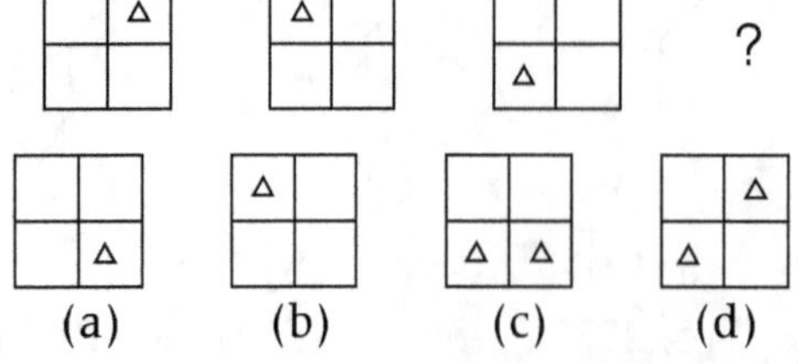

(a)　　(b)　　(c)　　(d)

23. Match the following pattern of shapes with the same pattern of alphabets.

Column A	Column B
A. △□○○□△△□○○□△	1. ABCAABCABBC ...
B. 1 2 3 1 2 3 1 2 3 1 2 3	2. PQRPPQQRR ...
C. ▨◐▲▨▨◐◐▲▲▲▨▨▨	3. XYZZYXXYZZYX ...
D. 1 2 3 1 1 2 3 1 2 2 3 ...	4. ABDABDABDABD

	A	B	C	D		A	B	C	D
(a)	1	4	3	2	(b)	3	4	2	1
(c)	4	3	2	1	(d)	2	1	4	3

24. A cat is chasing a mouse as shown below. The mouse is at 23 metres mark.

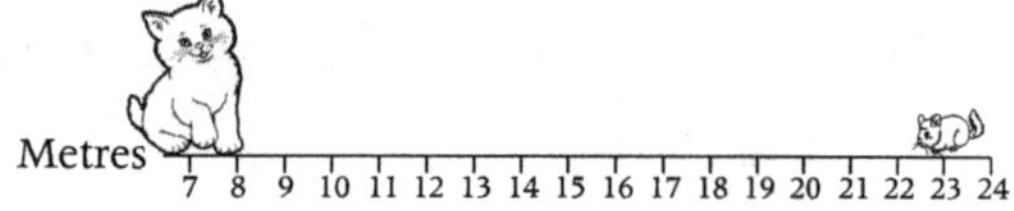

The cat starts from 7 m and jumps 4 m every time. How many jumps will the cat have to make to reach the mouse?

(a) 2　　(b) 4　　(c) 3　　(d) 5

25. State whether 'T' for true or 'F' for false.

1. Top view and side view of a cuboid are same.

2. 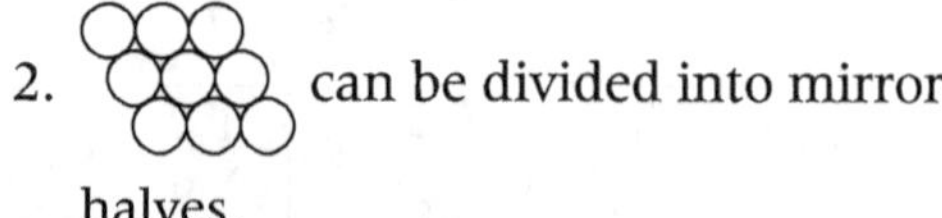 can be divided into mirror halves.

3. No letter in the name 'AMIT' can be divided into mirror halves.

4. ☂ is the top of view of an umbrella.

Codes

	1	2	3	4		1	2	3	4
(a)	F	T	F	F	(b)	T	T	F	T
(c)	F	F	T	F	(d)	T	T	F	F

Data Handling

Directions (Q.Nos. 1 and 2) Look at the following pictograph and answer the following questions carefully.

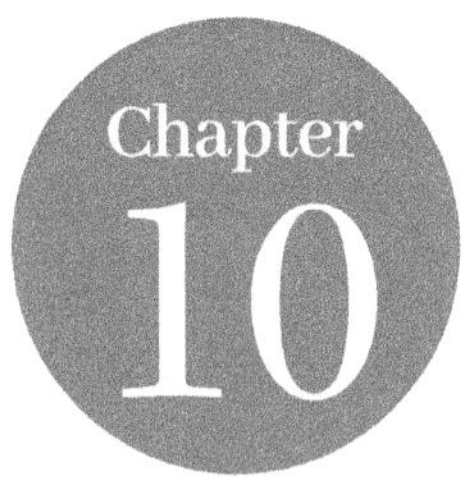

Favourite in Summer Vacation	
River boating	
Beach house	
Camping	
Big city	
Road trip	
Amusement park	

1. Number of children who choose road trip is equal to number of children who choose

   (a) Beach House   (b) River Boating

   (c) Camping   (d) Big city

2. Difference in the number of children who choose Amusement park and camping?

   (a) 3   (b) 10

   (c) 4   (d) 1

Directions (Q.Nos. 3 and 4) The given pictograph shows the number of pens each child bought. Use the given information and answer the following questions.

Number of pens bought by 4 children	
Madhav	
Achyut	
Krishna	
Govind	
Each stands for 10 pens.	

3. How many pens did the four children buy together?

   (a) 17   (b) 12

   (c) 16   (d) 170

4. If each pen costs ₹ 10, How much did Govind spend in all?

   (a) ₹ 400

   (b) ₹ 300

   (c) ₹ 800

   (d) ₹ 350

Directions (Q.Nos. 5 and 6) The bar graph shows the number of ice-creams 5 students have.

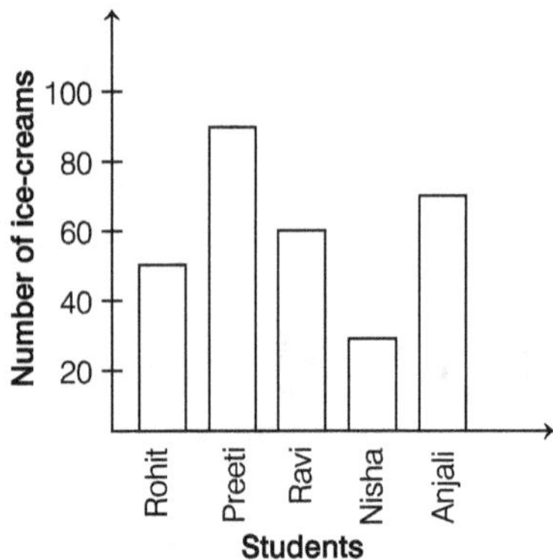

5. Who has twice ice-creams as Nisha has?
(a) Anjali
(b) Preeti
(c) Rohit
(d) Ravi

6. How many ice-creams did the students have altogether?
(a) 500
(b) 300
(c) 200
(d) 400

Directions (Q.Nos. 7 and 8) Study the following graph carefully and answer the questions that follows.

The given bar graph shows the amount spent by Jack on different items on a certain day.

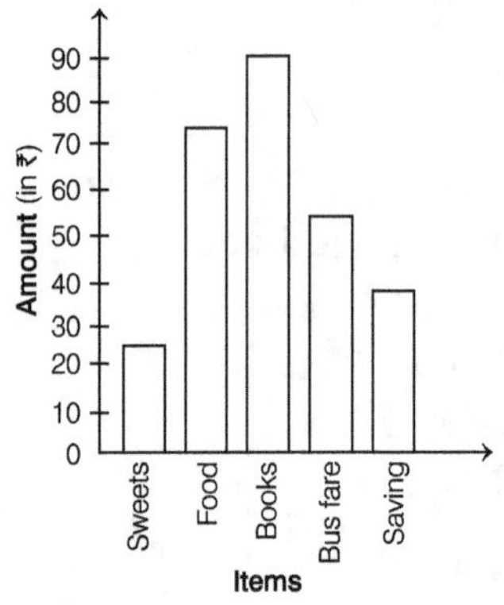

7. How much Jack would saved, if he had not bought the books?
(a) ₹ 75
(b) ₹ 55
(c) ₹ 90
(d) ₹ 25

8. How much more money did Jack spend on Books than on Bus fare?
(a) ₹ 30
(b) ₹ 50
(c) ₹ 140
(d) ₹ 35

Directions (Q.Nos. 9 and 10) The given table shows how many bags of popcorn sold in the past 4 days by Peter. Answer the following questions carefully.

Bags of popcorn should	
Day	**Number of bags of popcorn**
Wednesday	529
Thursday	585
Friday	582
Saturday	552

9. The difference between the maximum and minimum number of bags sold by peter in past 4 days?
(a) 56
(b) 58
(c) 65
(d) 85

10. The sum of total number of bags sold on Wednesday and Saturday together?
(a) 1080
(b) 1081
(c) 1083
(d) 1802

Directions (Q.Nos. 11 and 12) The given table shows the marks obtained by the students in a class. Answer the following questions carefully.

Student's name	Marks
Andrew	45
Amaira	36
Tony	32
Imaika	49
Samantha	56
Jeshua	50
David	53

11. The sum of the highest and lowest marks obtain by the students?

(a) 78

(b) 88

(c) 69

(d) 106

12. Who got the second highest marks?

(a) Jeshua

(b) Imaika

(c) Samantha

(d) David

13. 80 children visited the zoo. They each voted for their favourite animal.

Favourite animal		Number of votes
Cheetah	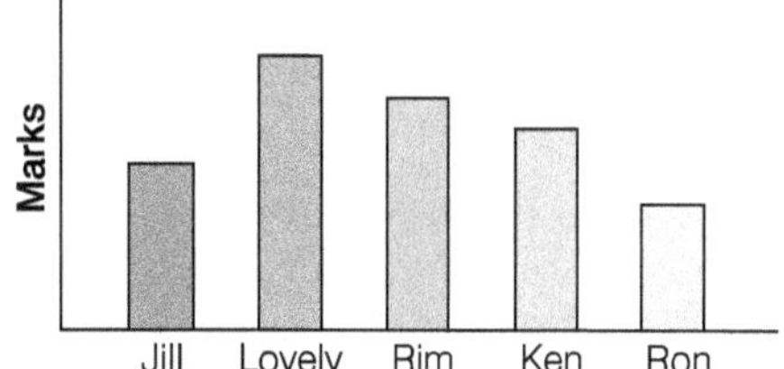	12
Lion		25
Tiger		18
Leopard		14
Panther		?
Total		80

How many children gave the vote for panther?

(a) 12   (b) 14

(c) 13   (d) 11

14. Five friends made a graph of the number of marks they got in mathematics.

What is the correct sequence of labels on the picture above in descending order?

(a) Lovely, Rim, Jill, Ken, Ron

(b) Rim, Jill, Lovely, Ron, Ken

(c) Lovely, Rim, Ken, Jill, Ron

(d) Ron, Ken, Rim, Lovely, Jill

Directions (Q.Nos. 15 and 16) Kristine counted the number of different types of cars in her colony. She made a graph to show the data.

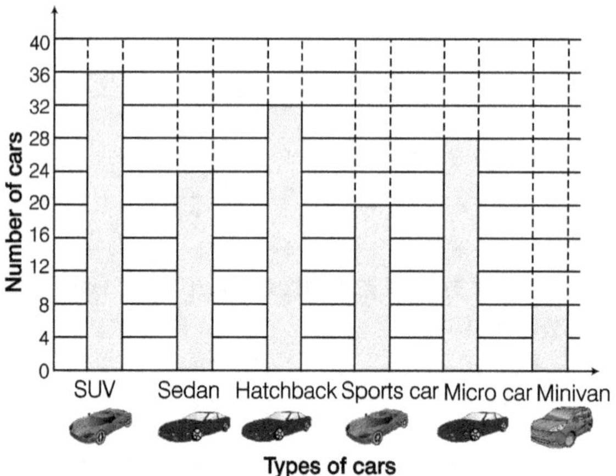

15. What is the total number of cars parked in Kratika's colony?

(a) 6   (b) 132

(c) 148   (d) 152

16. What is the difference between the maximum number and minimum number of cars parked?

(a) 8   (b) 36

(c) 28   (d) 24

17. Romela drew a graph showing the number of dresses of different colours she has.

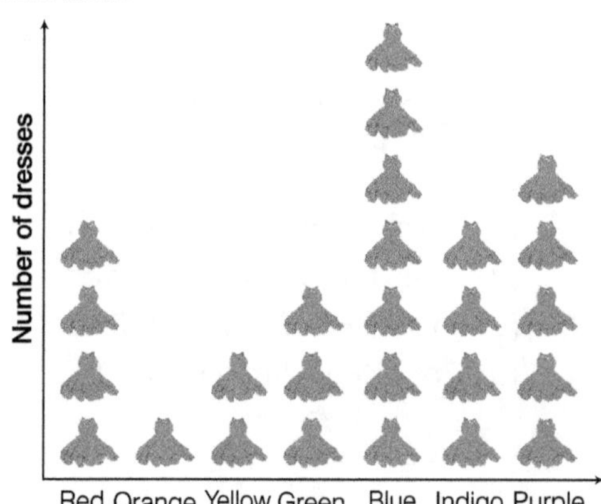

Which colour dress is 8 less than the purple coloured dress?

(a) Yellow

(b) Red

(c) Blue

(d) Orange

18. The given below chart shows the musical instruments, which some children play

Musical instruments	Lauren	Jane	Richard	Nainy	Yon
Drums	✓	✓		✓	
Keyboard			✓		
Trumpet	✓				✓
Recorder			✓	✓	✓
Piano	✓	✓	✓		

How many children play more than two musical instruments?

(a) 4   (b) 3

(c) 1   (d) 2

19. The given table shows the number of boys who were absent in a day of a particular week.

Day	Number of Boys
Monday	☺ ☺ ☺
Tuesday	☺ ☺ ☺ ☺
Wednesday	☺ ☺
Thursday	☺ ☺ ☺ ☺
Friday	☺ ☺ ☺ ☺ ☺
Saturday	☺
Each ☺ means 5 boys	

How many boys were absent on Thursday and Friday altogether?

(a) 45   (b) 36

(c) 9   (d) 10

20. Study the following diagram and answer the question that follows.

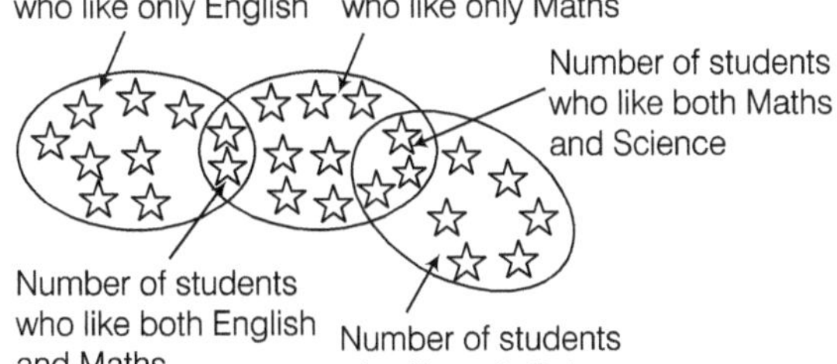

How many students like two subjects?

(a) 5

(b) 8

(c) 20

(d) 12

21. Dharampal watchman gets a duty of recording the number of bikes which are parked at the parking at different times on one day. He made a bar chart to show his recordings as given below.

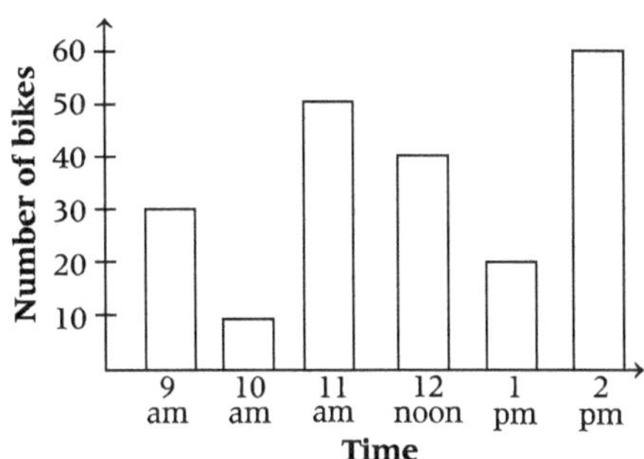

Read the bar chart and match the following:

List I	List II
A. 10 am	1. 60 bikes
B. 12 noon	2. 10 bikes
c. 2 pm	3. 40 bikes
D. 9 am	4. 30 bikes

       A B C D
(a) 1 3 4 2
(b) 4 1 3 2
(c) 3 1 2 4
(d) 2 3 1 4

PRACTICE SET 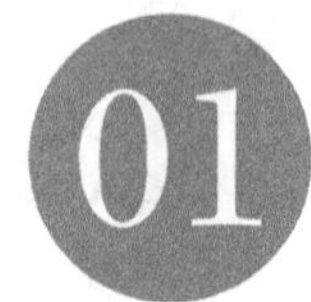 01

1. The difference between 954 hundred and x is 89290, then find the value of x.
   (a) 6000   (b) 5150
   (c) 7829   (d) 6110

2. Mr. Bharat distributed ₹ 11895 equally among 15 children. How much amount did two children get?
   (a) ₹ 1586   (b) ₹ 1400
   (c) ₹ 1846   (d) None of these

3. Kapil spends ₹ 120 to buy 6 lollipops and 3 candies. If lollipop costs ₹ 18 each, then find the cost of 1 such candy.
   (a) ₹ 5   (b) ₹ 4
   (c) ₹ 6   (d) ₹ 12

4. What is the weight of each apple?

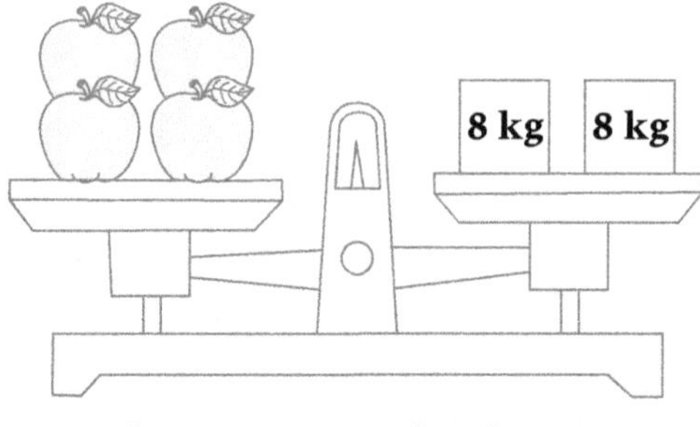

   (a) 4 kg   (b) 3 kg
   (c) 2 kg   (d) 1 kg

5. What fraction of the figure is shaded?

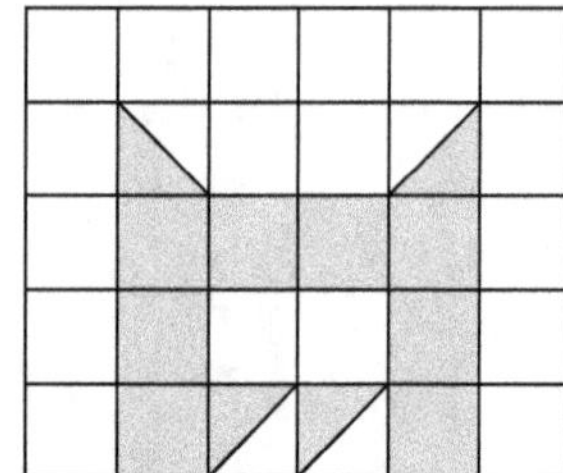

6. What number should be added to 8.439 to make it 3 times of 6.7?
   (a) 11.001
   (b) 11.661
   (c) 12.551
   (d) None of the above

   (a) $\dfrac{1}{2}$ (b) $\dfrac{7}{15}$
   (c) $\dfrac{17}{30}$ (d) $\dfrac{1}{3}$

7. Saurabh is 10 yr old and his father Mr. Subodh is 6 times as old as he is. If his mother Mrs. Neha is 3 yr younger than his father, then how old his mother is?
   (a) 55 yr   (b) 58 yr
   (c) 57 yr   (d) 59 yr

8. The given graph shows the number of toffees 5 students have.

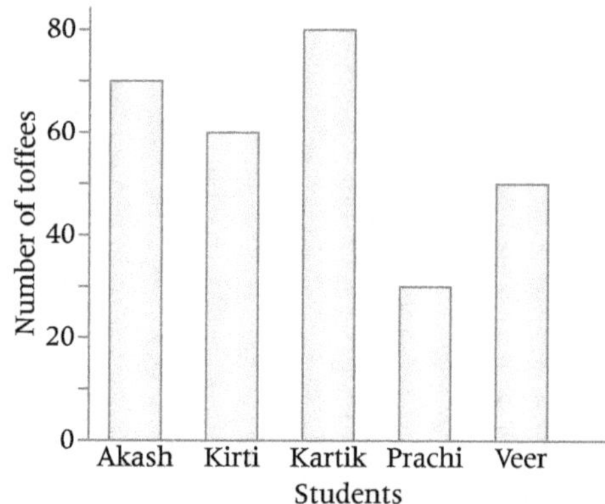

   How many more toffees does Kartik has than Akash?
   (a) 10   (b) 15
   (c) 20   (d) 30

9. The given clocks show the time at which a web series started and finished. How long was the web series?

(a) 2 h 30 min
(b) 1 h 45 min
(c) 1 h 40 min
(d) 1 h 25 min

10. How many hundreds are there in 97321 + 4057?

(a) 78   (b) 1300
(c) 3   (d) 5

11. Find the value of x in the given equation.
$$572 \times 3 \times 50 = x \times 52 \times 101$$
(a) 160
(b) 8
(c) 165
(d) None of the above

12. Match the shape of the following objects:

Column I	Column II
P. A Book	1. Cone
Q. Birthday hat	2. Rectangle
R. A Black-board	3. Cuboid
S. A Ball	4. Circle

	P	Q	R	S
(a)	2	4	1	3
(b)	3	2	1	4
(c)	4	2	1	3
(d)	3	1	2	4

13. What come next in the pattern?

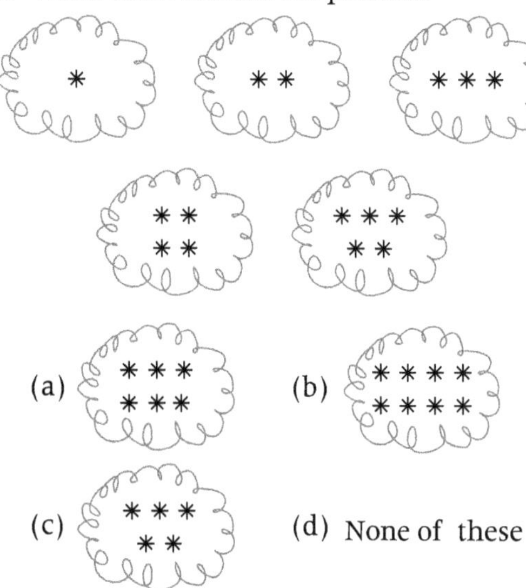

(a)   (b)

(c)   (d) None of these

14. If the digit at hundreds place is interchanged with the digit at tenth place of the number shown by the abacus, then find the difference between the new number and original number.

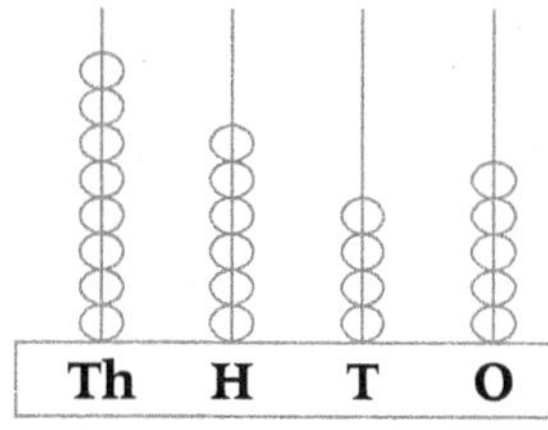

(a) 180   (b) 175
(c) 190   (d) 170

15. Taru bought 10 dozen of bananas. He gave 4 dozen bananas to his sister and used 6 bananas to make a shake. How many bananas were left with him?

(a) 75   (b) 76
(c) 65   (d) 66

16. Ben and Den were playing darts. Each one threw 4 darts and summed up the score (see the picture). Who won and by how many points did he win?

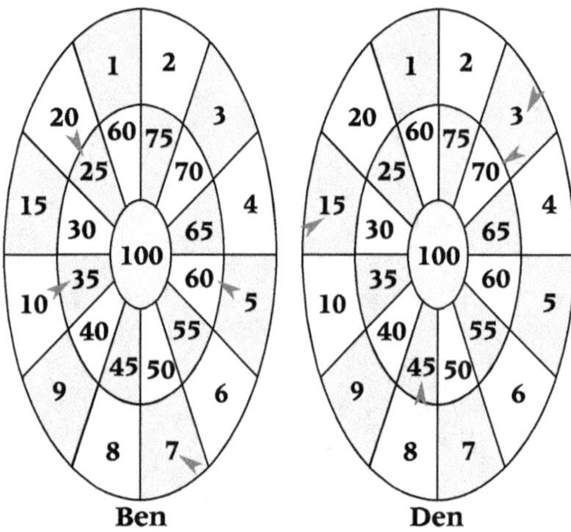

(a) Ben, 7 points
(b) Den, 6 points
(c) Ben, 5 points
(d) Den, 8 points

17. A woman bought a total of 122 packets of milk in the month of June and July together. If she bought equal number of packets on each day, then how many packets of milk woman buy in June?

(a) 55   (b) 60
(c) 63   (d) 72

18. Sonu and Monu had gone to jeans corner and bought two jeans on 1+1 offer for ₹1200.

1+1 offer
Buy 1 get 1 free

If both of them pair equal amount. Find the amount paid by each.

(a) ₹ 650   (b) ₹ 600
(c) ₹ 550   (d) ₹ 500

19. A ladder is 7 m 50 cm high. Navya has climbed 4 m 25 cm. How much more does she need to climb to reach the top?

(a) 3 m 25 cm
(b) 2 m 50 cm
(c) 1 m 25 cm
(d) 4 m 50 cm

Directions (Q. Nos. 20-21) Lauren asked her friends what their favourite animal was and then made a pictogram to show her results.

Favourite animals	
Cats	🐱🐱🐱
Lions	🦁🦁🦁🦁🦁
Dogs	🐕🐕🐕🐕🐕🐕🐕
Horses	🐎🐎🐎🐎🐎🐎🐎🐎
Giraffes	🦒🦒🦒
Others	? ? ? ? ? ?

1 icon = 3 person's favourite animal
On the basis of above information, answer the questions that follow.

20. Which animals is liked by 15 people?
(a) Others   (b) Lion
(c) Dog   (d) Cat

21. Which animals is liked by 6 more people than the category of other animals?
(a) Horse   (b) Dogs
(c) Giraffes   (d) Lion

22. What are the missing number in the pattern?

29, 31, 35, 37, 41, ?, 47, ?

(a) 43, 49   (b) 45, 50
(c) 44, 46   (d) 46, 48

23. Shubhi is 16 cm taller than Karishma. Stuti is 6 cm shorter than Anshu. Karishma and Stuti are same of height. If Anshu is 159 cm tall, then height of Shubhi is
  (a) 160 cm   (b) 158 cm
  (c) 170 cm   (d) 169 cm

24. How many hours and minutes are there in 350 minutes?
  (a) 6 h 40 min   (b) 4 h 30 min
  (c) 5 h 30 min   (d) 6 h 30 min

25. Which of the following figures has only 3 faces?

(a)    (b) 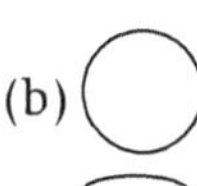

(c) 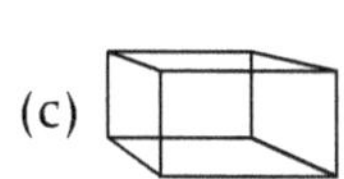   (d) 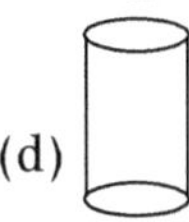

  (a) Club   (b) Hospital
  (c) School   (d) Mall

26. Mr. Abhishek class went to the zoo on the 5th Sunday in November, 2020. On what date did his class go to the zoo?

November 2020						
SUN	MON	TUS	WED	THU	FRI	SAT
1	2	3	4	5	6	7
8	9	10	11	12	13	14
15	16	17	18	19	20	21
22	23	24	25	26	27	28
29	30					

  (a) November 22   (b) November 29
  (c) November 30   (d) November 28

27. On the basis of the given figure, select the CORRECT statement.

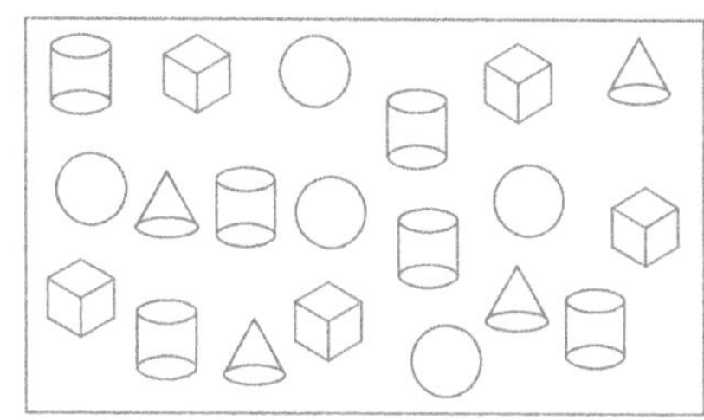

  (a) $\dfrac{5}{20}$ of total shapes are cubes

  (b) $\dfrac{6}{15}$ of total shapes are cylinders

  (c) $\dfrac{3}{20}$ of total shapes are circles

  (d) All of the above

28. Find the value: $4.3 \times 6 \times 0.25$
  (a) 6.05   (b) 6.45
  (c) 6.50   (d) 7.05

29. Select the correct ascending order.
  (a) 4 m 30 cm, 5 m 20 cm, 5 m 22 cm, 6 m
  (b) 3 L 330 mL, 500 mL, 2 L 20 mL, 750 mL
  (c) 900 g, 1 kg 200 g, 2 kg 350 g, 1500 g
  (d) None of the above

30. Study the given figure carefully and find the value of 'A'.

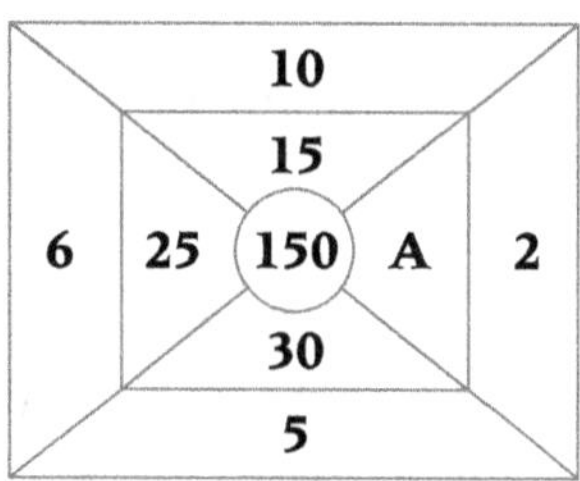

  (a) 70   (b) 75
  (c) 60   (d) 50

31. Harsh sold 125 burgers and 90 spring rolls. If Nitin sold 20 less burgers and 10 less spring rolls than Harsh, then how many burgers and springs rolls they sold together?

(a) 225 burgers and 170 spring rolls.

(b) 250 burgers and 170 springs rolls.

(c) 230 burgers and 170 springs rolls.

(d) 130 burgers and 190 spring rolls.

Direction (Q. No. 32) Use the table given below to answer the question.

Tours of Australia

Tours last about 4 h and 15 min	
Bus	**Departure time**
Red coach	9 : 45 am
Blue coach	11 : 25 am
Green coach	1 : 40 pm
Yellow coach	3 : 15 pm
Orange coach	4 : 00 pm

32. The potter family is seeing a Broadway show at 5 : 30 pm. Which of the given tours can they take?

(a) Blue coach   (b) Green coach

(c) Orange coach   (d) Yellow coach

33. Yojana travelled the distance of 1028 km by three modes of transport. She travelled 1/2 distance by bus, 1/2 of left distance by car and rest by walking. Find the distance by walking.

(a) 342 km   (b) 420 km

(c) 257 km   (d) 513 km

34. Study the given figures carefully and find the weight of

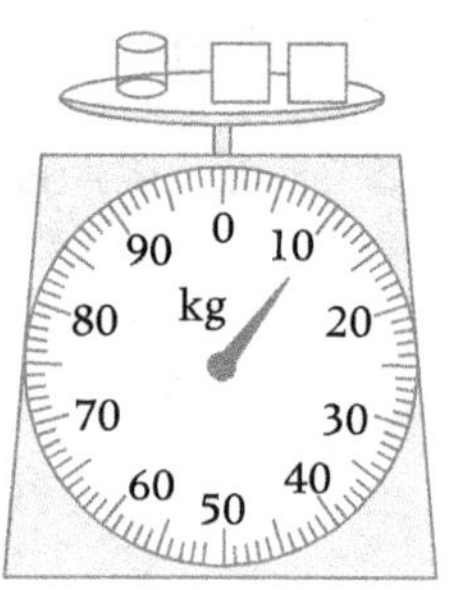
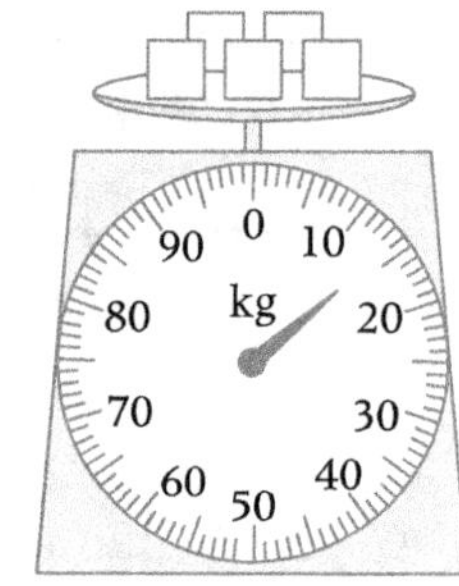

(a) 15 kg   (b) 18 kg   (c) 22 kg   (d) 10 kg

35. Six friends went for shopping. They bought the following items.

Alka	**Anubhav**	**Sunny**
Shoes-₹375	Belt-₹185	Shoes-₹180
Jeans-₹590	Shirt-₹470	Jacket-₹690
Bellies-₹460	Jacket-₹745	Jeans-₹466

Nisha	**Astha**	**Akshat**
Jeans-₹550	Shirt-₹315	Jeans-₹745
Jackets-₹425	Saree-₹766	Shirt-₹355
Heels-₹375	Jeans-₹240	Belt-₹145

On the basis of the given information, fill in the blanks.

1. ..... spent the least amount.

2. .... spent ₹ 1321 on shopping.

3. Sunny spent .... on shopping.

4. ..... spent the most amount.

	1	2	3	4
(a)	Akshat	Astha	₹ 1336	Alka
(b)	Nisha	Astha	₹ 1400	Sunny
(c)	Alka	Sunny	₹ 1336	Anubhav
(d)	Sunny	Alka	₹ 1425	Akshat

PRACTICE SET 02

1. This mirror is about 15 buttons long. About how many safety pins long is the mirror?

(a) 4
(c) 5
(b) 12
(d) 10

2.

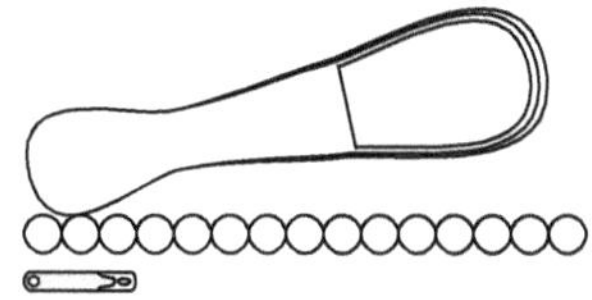
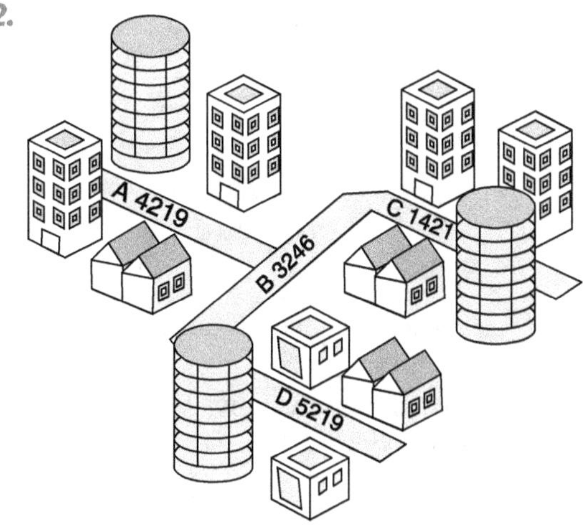

Which streets number given in the above map have '2' in the hundred's place?

(a) B. A and C
(b) A, B and D
(c) A, C and B
(d) A, D and C

3. Mia used blocks to build the model of her dog's kennel.

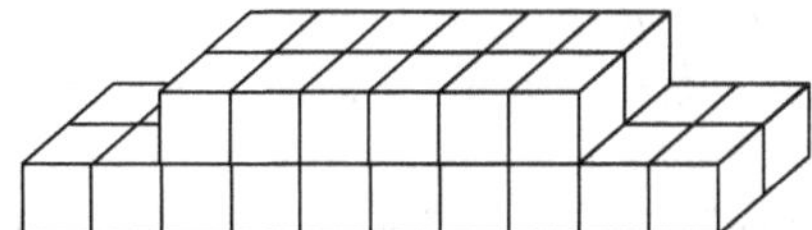

Which building does Mia's model represent.

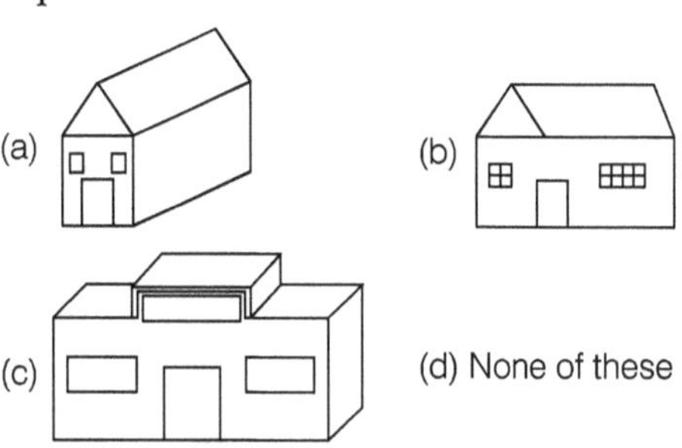

4. Romela is playing a guessing game with her friends. When they say 5, she says 20. When they say 9, she says 36. When they say 12, she says 48. What would she say, if her friends said 29?

(a) 33   (b) 116   (c) 120   (d) 35

5. Elena drove her car on two days. She drove a total of 12 kilometres in two days. On the first day, Elena drove $\frac{5}{6}$ of the total distance. How many kilometres did she drove on the second day?

(a) 10 kilometres   (b) 12 kilometres
(c) 6 kilometres   (d) 2 kilometres

6. Study the following pattern of stars.

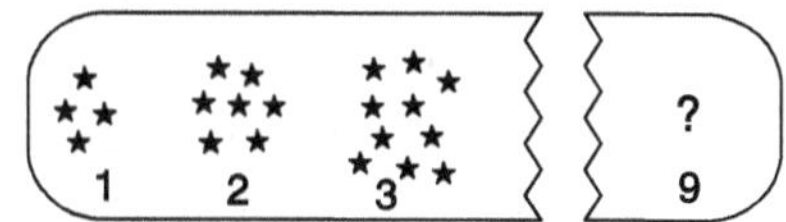

How many stars made the 9th figure, before the paper was cut?

(a) 21
(c) 28
(b) 25
(d) 31

7. Amantha puts fruit slices on a tray.
   She puts 40 apple slices on a tray.
   She puts 12 fewer pear slices than apple slices on the tray.
   What is the number of pear slices □ on the tray?
   (a) □ − 40 = 12
   (b) □ − 12 = 40
   (c) 40 − 12 = □
   (d) None of these

8. These scales show how much a glass weighs alone and how much it weighs with a cup. How many grams would the cup weigh without the glass?

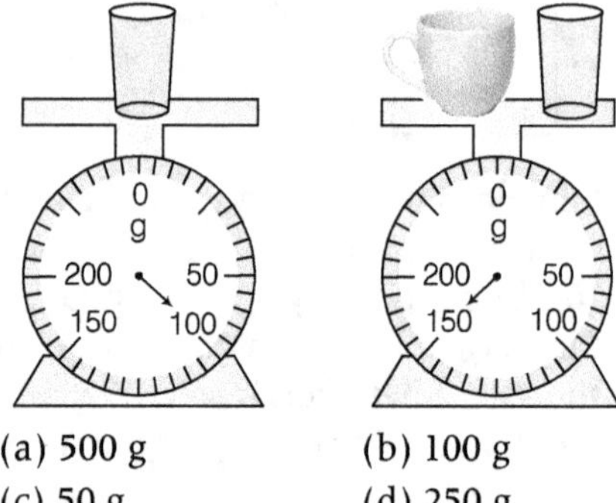

   (a) 500 g
   (b) 100 g
   (c) 50 g
   (d) 250 g

9. Amantha made 134 cupcakes for her birthday party. The cupcakes were divided into boxes having 11 cupcakes each. What was the total number of boxes and the total number of cupcakes left over?
   (a) 10 boxes, 3 cupcakes left
   (b) 12 boxes, 2 cupcakes left
   (c) 13 boxes, 1 cupcake left
   (d) 11 boxes, 4 cupcakes left

10. Elle was staring across the street, where bicycle and tricycle were parked. She counted a total of 13 wheels. How many two wheelers and three wheelers were in the lot?
    (a) 3 bicycles and 2 tricycles
    (b) 5 bicycles and 1 tricycle
    (c) 4 bicycles and 1 tricycle
    (d) 3 bicycles and 4 tricycles

11. Beny is using three cards shown below to make a three-digit number. Which list shows all the possible 3-digit numbers. Beny can make using each card, if repetition of cards, is not allowed?

    | 5 | 6 | 3 |

    (a) 365, 653, 563
    (b) 365, 356, 653, 536
    (c) 365, 356, 635, 653, 536, 563
    (d) 365, 356, 635, 653, 536, 563, 555, 333, 666

12. ✓, ★, ✳ and ☼ each stands for a digit. Find what each stands for using these clues.

    $$\begin{array}{c} ☼\ ✓ \\ -\ ★\ ✳ \\ \hline 2\ 1 \end{array} \qquad \begin{array}{c} ✳ \\ +\ ✳ \\ \hline 10 \end{array} \qquad \begin{array}{c} ✓ \\ +\ ✳ \\ \hline 11 \end{array} \qquad \begin{array}{c} ☼ \\ +\ ☼ \\ \hline 8 \end{array}$$

    Codes

	☼	✳	✓	★		☼	✳	✓	★
(a)	4	5	8	12	(b)	8	10	16	8
(c)	4	5	6	2	(d)	10	12	12	4

13. City school collects money for three charities.

    This pictogram shows how much they have collected.

    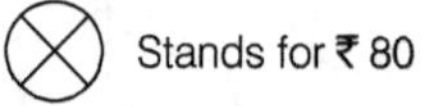 Stands for ₹ 80

Girl's education	⊗	⊗	⊗	◖	
Old age people	⊗	⊗	◗		
Plant a tree	⊗	⊗	⊗		

    How much more money have they collected for girl's education than old age people?
    (a) ₹ 100   (b) ₹ 180   (c) ₹ 280   (d) ₹ 460

Directions (Q. Nos. 14 and 15)
'Revolutionary' group of people performing short films have different sessions of films given below

Camp windes	
Session 1	July 13-July 17
Session 2	July 27-July 31
Session 3	August 1-August 14

14. The film director bought art supplies 2 weeks before the beginning of the first session. On what date did she buy art supplies?
(a) 1st July   (b) 25th June
(c) 27th July   (d) 29th June

15. The day on which third session started is Monday. In session 3, the group put on a broadway show on the second Wednesday of the session. What was the date of the broadway show?
(a) 3rd August   (b) 10th August
(c) 8th August   (d) 14th August

16. Jeff planted 6 rows of rose plants with 5 plants in each row. She put 3 more plants in another row. What is the total number of plants she put?
(a) $6 + 3 + 5$ (b) $(6 \times 3) + 5$
(c) $(6 \times 5) + 3$ (d) $6 \times 5 \times 3$

17. Jeshua's clue about his mystery number is shown in the box. What is Jeshua's mystery number?

My number has
7 tens
4 thousands
3 ones
2 ten thousands
0 hundreds

(a) 2473   (b) 20473   (c) 24730   (d) 24073

18. Monty has stickers in his box. He took one sticker out of his box without looking. He got stickers with stars on it. What is the fraction of such stickers he has in his box?

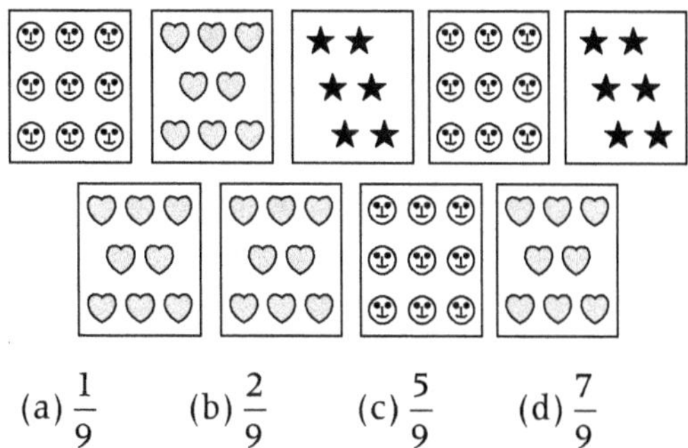

(a) $\dfrac{1}{9}$ (b) $\dfrac{2}{9}$ (c) $\dfrac{5}{9}$ (d) $\dfrac{7}{9}$

19. What will come next in the sequence?

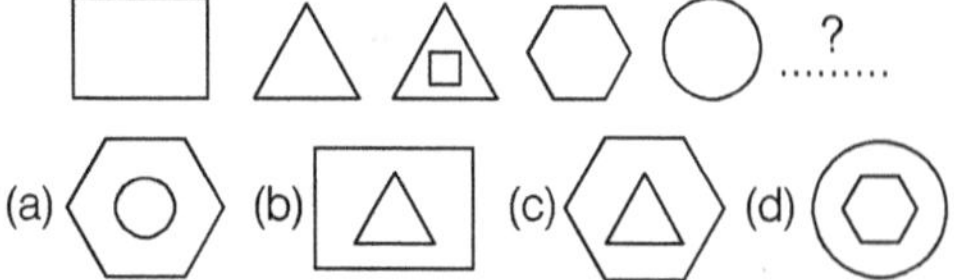

(a)   (b)   (c)   (d)

20. A cake was divided into 15 pieces. Emily ate $\dfrac{1}{5}$ of the pieces. Tenzen ate $\dfrac{2}{5}$ of the pieces. Jaun ate $\dfrac{1}{5}$ of the pieces. What fraction of pieces was left?
(a) 10   (b) 6   (c) 3   (d) 5

21. Linda travelled from town Z to town X and Andrew travelled from town Y to town W. Who travelled a longer distance and by how much?

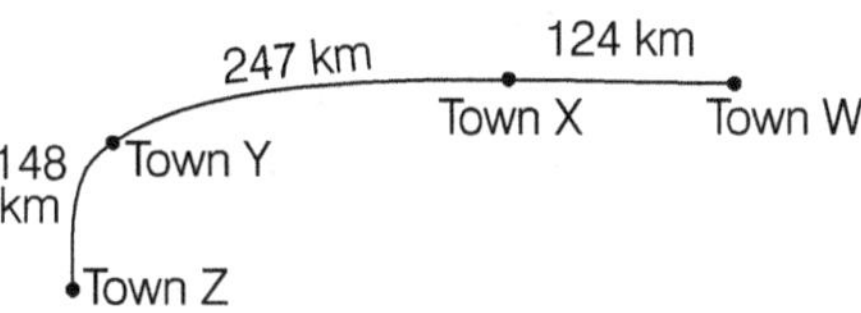

(a) Andrew, 48 km   (b) Linda, 24 km
(c) Linda, 36 km   (d) None of these

22. Look at the picture below

Which of the following statement is true?

(a) Number of triangles is equal to number of circles

(b) Number of rectangles is less than number of triangles

(c) Number of triangles is less than number of rectangles

(d) Number of circles is equal to number of rectangles

23. The below table shows the distance from Boston to different cities

To city	Number of miles
Kansas city	1391
Phila delphia	296
Houstan	1804

What is the distance from Boston to Houstan?

(a) one thousand eight hundred four miles

(b) one hundred eighty four

(c) one thousand 8 tens 4 ones

(d) None of the above

24. Mr. Brown's family went to a nearby beach for picnic.

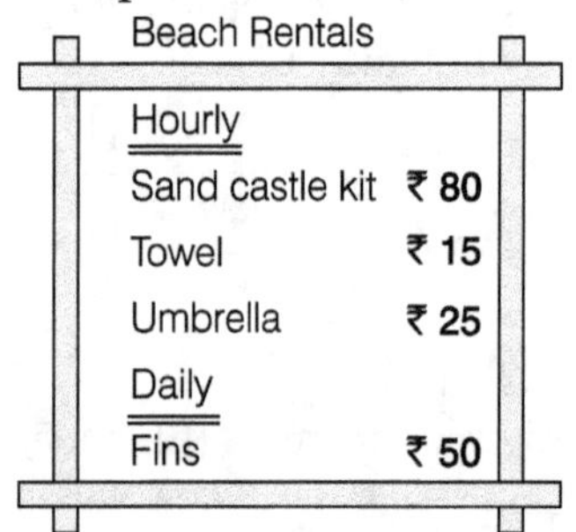

Mr. Brown's family took a sand castle kit, a towel for 3 hours on rent.

How much did it cost to them?

(a) ₹ 240   (b) ₹ 45   (c) ₹ 195   (d) ₹ 285

25. Juan bought 180 stickers. He bought $\dfrac{4}{9}$ of the total stickers of pokemon and remaining stickers are of spiderman. How many stickers of spiderman he bought?

(a) 100   (b) 80   (c) 180   (d) 200

26. Look at the top two scales. How many pencils would balance three balls?

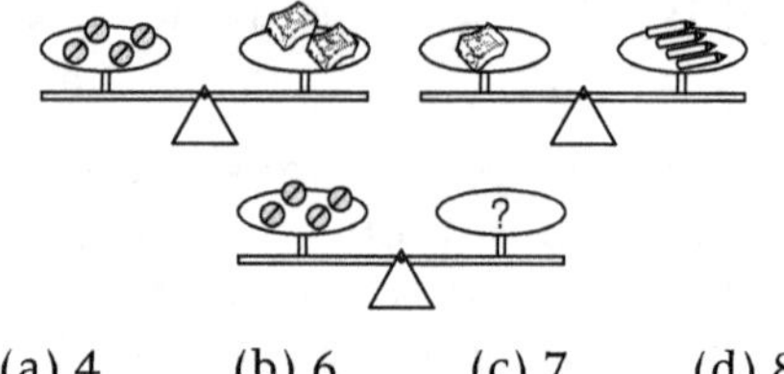

(a) 4   (b) 6   (c) 7   (d) 8

27. There are 21 girls and 18 boys in each section of class 4. How many students are there in 5 such sections?

(a) 155   (b) 195

(c) 39   (d) 44

28. What fraction of the figure is shaded?

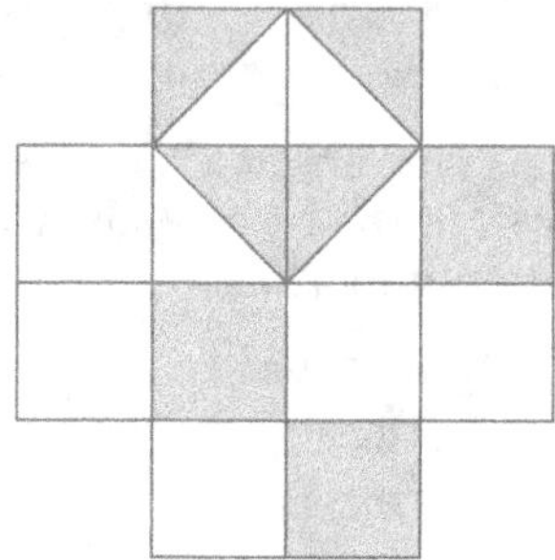

(a) $\dfrac{5}{12}$ (b) $\dfrac{7}{12}$

(c) $\dfrac{9}{12}$ (d) $\dfrac{11}{12}$

29. A group of pupils shared 108 stamps. 5 of them shared a total of 44 stamps. The rest had 8 stamps each. How many pupils were there altogether?

(a) 5 (b) 13
(c) 18 (d) 8

30. If Mayank go on a movie on 8th date of the month, then what will be the day after 2 weeks and 3 days.

June 2018						
SUN	MON	TUE	WED	THU	FRI	SAT
					1	2
3	4	5	6	7	8	9
10	11	12	13	14	15	16
17	18	19	20	21	22	23
24	25	26	27	28	29	30

(a) Sunday
(b) Friday
(c) Monday
(d) Wednesday

31. Match the shape of the following object:

List-I	List-II
A. A Dice	1. Circle
B. A Bottle Cap	2. Cuboid
C. A Black-board	3. Cube
D. A Pencil box	4. Rectangle

Codes

	A	B	C	D
(a)	4	3	2	1
(b)	2	3	1	4
(c)	1	2	3	4
(d)	3	1	4	2

32. Aakash needs to buy an chocolate worth ₹ 5. He has some coins of 10p, 25p and 50p. Which of the following combination of coins will help him in buying the chocolate?

(a) 5 coins of 10p, 8 coins of 25p and 4 coins of 50p
(b) 10 coins of 10p, 12 coins of 25p and 1 coin of 50 p
(c) 10 coins of 10p, 12 coins of 25p and 2 coins of 50 p
(d) 20 coins of 10p, 4 coins of 25p and 3 coins of 50p

33. Which of the following is the same as 125 sec?

(a) 2 min 5 sec (b) 1 min 5 sec
(c) 3 min 5 sec (d) 12 min 5 sec

34. If you have ₹ 1500. How much money will be left with you. If you buy one pair of shoes, two pair of socks and one belt?

Shoes—₹ 550 each pair
Socks—₹ 80 each pair
Belt ₹ 150

(a) ₹ 205 (b) ₹ 191
(c) ₹ 540 (d) ₹ 640

35. The first session of a cricket match began at 8 : 15 am. If lasted for 3 h and 30 min.

When did the first session end?
(a) 8 : 45 am (b) 10 : 45 am
(c) 12 : 45 pm (d) 11 : 45 am

Hints & Solutions

Chapter 1 : Numbers

1. *(c)* We have, the length of bridge as

Option (a), **2740** → Thousand's place

Option (b), **2730** → Thousand's place

Option (c), **1261** → Hundred's place

Option (d),

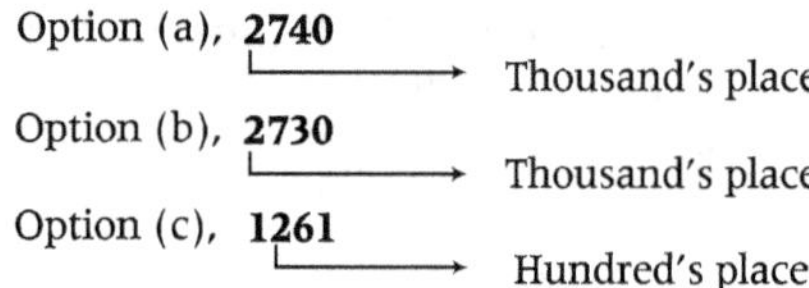

So, option (c) is correct.

2. *(d)* The number which Deepa likes has same digits at unit's place and hundred's place. So, Deepa will like the number 696.

3. *(d)* Since the digits are same at thousands and hundred'th place in both the number, therefore to determine the larger number, we have to compare digits at tens place.

4. *(b)* The number shown by the beads in the abacus $= 3 \times 100 + 2 \times 10 + 4 \times 1$
$$= 300 + 20 + 4 = 324$$
Now, adding two more beads at hundred's bar will make the number
$$= 500 + 20 + 4 = 524$$

5. *(b)* A → Predecessor of smallest 4-digit number
$$= 1000 - 1 = 999$$
B → Successor of greatest 3-digit number
$$= 999 + 1 = 1000$$
C → Successor of smallest 4-digit even number $= 1000 + 1$
$$= 1001$$
D → Predecessor of greatest 4-digit odd number $= 9999 - 1 = 9998$
So, $\qquad$ D > C > B > A
Hence, bag D has the greatest number of coins.

6. *(d)* We have, the number entered is
$$7290 = 7000 + 200 + 90 + 0$$
$$= 7 \times 1000 + 2 \times 100 + 9 \times 10 + 0 \times 1$$
$$= 7 \text{ thousand } 2 \text{ hundred } 9 \text{ tens}$$
$$= 7 \text{ thousand } 2 \text{ hundred } 90 \text{ ones}$$
$$[\text{as } 9 \text{ tens} = 90 \text{ ones}]$$

7. *(d)* We can write, nine thousand eight hundred seventy six $= 9876 = 9000 + 800 + 70 + 6$

8. *(a)* A. $200 + 70 + 9 = 279$
B. $2000 + 700 + 90 = 2790$
C. $200 + 9 = 209$
D. $2000 + 70 + 9 = 2079$
$\therefore$ A → 3, $\quad$ B → 2, $\quad$ C → 4, $\quad$ D → 1

9. *(c)* Given,

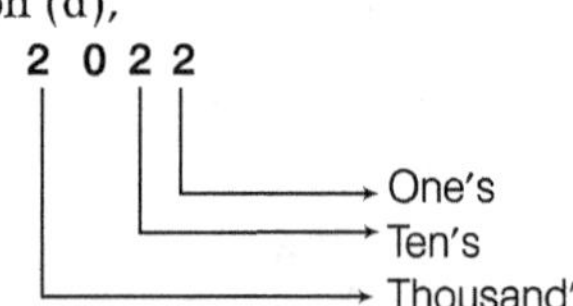

So,
$$= 4 \times 1000 + 3 \times 100 + 0 \times 10 + 4 \times 1$$
$$= 4000 + 300 + 0 + 4 = 4304$$

10. *(b)*

1. 50 tens + 40 ones
$$= 50 \times 10 + 40 \times 1$$
$$= 500 + 40 = 540$$

2. Least 5-digit number $= 10000$
Predecessor $= 10000 - 1 = 9999$

3. The number having '0' in tens place, 4 in hundred's place, 5 in ones place is 405.

4. The given model $= 200 + 30 + 6 = 236$
$\therefore$ 1 → E, $\quad$ 2 → H, $\quad$ 3 → G, $\quad$ 4 → A

11. *(c)* Considering each option, we have
In option (a), Number of pots $= 147$ (odd)
$\qquad\qquad$ Number of balls $= 329$ (odd)
In option (b), Number of pots $= 246$ (even)
$\qquad\qquad$ Number of balls $= 348$ (even)
In option (c), Number of pots $= 148$ (even)
$\qquad\qquad$ Number of balls $= 243$ (odd)
In option (d), Number of pots $= 249$ (odd)
$\qquad\qquad$ Number of balls $= 332$ (even)
So, only option (c) has odd number of balls and even number of pots.

12. *(b)* Mr. Daniel's changed house number $= 5427$
Mr. Addison's changed house number $= 4336$
Mr. Brick's changed house number $= 5777$
Mr. Andrew's changed house number $= 3223$
So, Mr. Addison's house number is an even number.

13. *(a)*

1. False, smallest three-digit odd number is 101.

2. False, 30 tens $= 300$

3. True,

T	H	T	O
8	2	3	4

= 3's place value is tens.

4. False, greatest 3 digit odd number.
$$= 999 = 1000 - 1$$

14. *(d)*

- As we know, the number is odd. So, the digit at one's place is 1, 3, 5, 7 or 9.
- Greatest one digit number is 9. So, at ten's place 9 will come.
- Digit at hundred's place is one more than digit at one's place.
- Digit at thousand's place is 2 less than ten's digit i.e., 7.
  Now, considering option (d), number 7493 satisfied the all conditions.

Hence, option (d) is correct.

15. *(d)* Given, score of Mahanta $= 1876$

and   score of Shampy $= 1654$

∵ Score of Shampy < Score of Mandy

< Score of Mahanta

[given]

Here, we see that

From option (a), $1654 < 1856 < 1876$

From option (b), $1654 < 1692 < 1876$

From option (c), $1654 < 1776 < 1876$

But 1653 given in option (d) is less than 1654.

So, the score of Mandy cannot be equal to 1653.

16. *(b)* We have, the numbers in descending order as follows.

(b)	(a)	(d)	(c)
8760 >	7517 >	5500 >	3653

So, greatest number is 8760.

Hence, option (b) is the statement with greatest number.

17. *(d)* The ascending order of the given scores is

Andy   Dondi   Ruby   Rizuk

$949 < 1001 < 1282 < 1426$

So, Ruby scored the second highest points.

18. *(c)* Arranging the almirahs in ascending order of their prices, we get

₹ 5624 < ₹ 5635 < ₹ 5645 < ₹ 5700

So, the arrangement given in option (c) is correct.

19. *(d)* Ascending order means that smallest to largest.

So, the correct sequence is

1320, 1451, 7912, 9568, 9658

20. *(d)* For the given statements to be true, we have the ink blot in Statement A must be less than 6, ink blot in Statement B must be greater than 5 and ink blot in Statement C must be equal to 4.

So,   A → 4,   B → 7,   C → 4

21. *(c)* Cost of blue colour skirt
$$= 4 \times 100 + 2 \times 10 + 4 \times 1 = 424$$
Cost of green colour skirt
$$= 1 \times 1000 + 2 \times 100 + 4 \times 10 = 1240$$
Cost of pink colour skirt $= 3 \times 100 + 2 = 302$
Cost of orange colour skirt
$$= 2 \times 100 + 9 \times 10 + 9 = 299$$
Arranging the cost of skirts in ascending order,
$$299 < 302 < 424 < 1240$$
So, we get orange skirt is the cheapest.

22. *(b)* Given number is 6013.

Arranging the digits in ascending order, we get
$$0 < 1 < 3 < 6$$
Now, 0 cannot be at thousand's place as a four-digit number is to be formed.

Hence, the smallest 4-digit number formed by using the above digits is 1036.

23. *(c)*   Jatin → 4434

Sonali → 4544

Ravi → 3151

Neha → 5163

The correct descending order is

Neha > Sonali > Jatin > Ravi

24. *(a)* Considering option (a):

6 2 3 1

A B C D

$A + B + D = 6 + 2 + 1 = 9$ (verified)

∴ *A* is 2 times of *C*.

$A = 6, C = 3$

So, $3 \times 2 = 6$ (verified)

∴ *B* is two times of *D*.

$B = 2, D = 1$

So, $1 \times 2 = 2$ (verified)

All conditions are full filled.

Hence, option (a) is correct.

25. *(a)* For train A, digit at ones place = 3

Digit at hundred's place $= 3 + 2 = 5$

Digit at ten's place $= 5 + 3 = 8$

So, number of passengers in train A $= 583$

For train B, digit at ten's place $= 2$

Digit at one's place $= 4 + 2 = 6$

Digit at hundred's place $= 6 - 2 = 4$

So, number of passengers in train B $= 426$

Now, $426 < 583$

Hence, train A is carrying more number of passengers than train B.

Chapter 2 : Addition and Subtraction

1. *(d)* By adding 3724 and 4397, we get

$$3724 + 4397 = \mathbf{8121}$$

where 8 → Thousand, 1 → Tens, 2 → Ones, 1 → Hundred

So, 1 on the hundred place.

2. *(c)* Given digits, 7, 6, 9, 2
Smallest 4-digit number made by given digit
= Digit should be arranged in ascending order.
i.e., → 2679.
Greatest 4-digit number made by given digit
= Digits should be arranged in descending order.
i.e., → 9762
Now, according to the question,
Greatest 4-digit number is subtracted from
smallest 4-digit number made by given digit.
i.e., → 9762 − 2679 = 7083

3. *(c)* Consider the unit digit in both number on
LHS, so 9 + 0 = 9.
Consider the ten's digit in both the number on
LHS.
Now, 4 will be added to a number will gives
result 7 i.e., on RHS.
So, correct option is (c).

4. *(a)* Distance covered from London to UK
$$= 674 \text{ km}$$
Distance covered from UK to Swindon = 468 km
So, total distance covered while travelling from
London to Swindon = Distance covered from
London to UK + Distance covered from UK to
Swindon = 674 + 468 = 1142 km

5. *(b)* On adding 1629 + 7465, we get
$$1629 + 7465 = 9094$$
Convert 9094 into expanded form, we get
$$9 \times 1000 + 0 \times 100 + 9 \times 10 + 4$$
We can also write it in number name as,
Nine thousand Ninety four.
[we don't write zero hundred]

6. *(c)* In a parking,
Number of blue cars = 873
Number of white cars = 1317
Number of red cars = 127 + Number of blue cars
$$= 127 + 873 = 1000$$
Total number of cars = Number of red cars
+ Number of white cars
+ Number of blue cars
$$= 1000 + 1317 + 873$$
$$= 2317 + 873 = 3190$$

7. *(a)* Number obtained in Step 1 = 300
Number obtained in Step 2 = 90
Number obtained in Step 3 = 11
So, Step 4 = Sum of numbers obtained in
Step 1, Step 2 and Step 3 = 300 + 90 + 11

8. *(b)* Given, $\qquad 7 + 2 = 9$
$$70 + 20 = 90$$
So, $\qquad 700 + \boxed{200} = 900 \qquad \qquad ...(i)$
and $\qquad \boxed{7000} + 2000 = 9000 \qquad ...(ii)$
Given, $\qquad 700 + \text{☺} = 900 \qquad \qquad ...(iii)$
On comparing Eqs. (i) and (iii), we get
$$\text{☺} = 200$$
Given, $\text{☺} + 2000 = 9000 \qquad \qquad ...(iv)$
Also, comparing Eqs. (ii) and (iv), we get
$$\text{☺} = 7000$$
∴ $\qquad \text{☺} + \text{☺} = 200 + 7000$
$$= 7000 + 200 = 7200$$
So, option (b) is correct.

9. *(d)* Least 5-digit number = 10000
Greatest 4-digit number = 9999
So, the number to be subtracted from least
5-digit number to get the greatest 4-digit
number = 10000 − 9999 = 1

10. *(b)* In a village,
Number of men = 2100
Number of women = 2450
∴ Number of women more than men
= Number of women − Number of men.
$$= 2450 − 2100 = 350$$

11. *(b)* Subtract 30 from each term to get next term.
$$340 − 30 = 310;$$
$$310 − 30 = \boxed{280}; \text{ (i)}$$
$$280 − 30 = 250;$$
$$250 − 30 = \boxed{220}; \text{ (ii)}$$
So, missing numbers are is 280, 220.
$\qquad\qquad\qquad\qquad\qquad$ (i) $\quad$ (ii)

12. *(a)* The number represented by the abacus
$$= 5 \times 1000 + 4 \times 100 + 3 \times 10 + 6 \times 1$$
$$= 5000 + 400 + 30 + 6 = 5436$$
Now, new number formed by interchanging the
digits at hundred's and one's place,
we get = 5634
So, difference between new and original
number = 5634 − 5436 = 198

13. *(a)* In a market,
Ruby bought vegetables of ₹ 240.
Note she gave to shopkeeper is ₹ 2000.
Change return by shopkeeper to Ruby is
$$= 2000 − 240 = ₹ 1760$$

14. *(d)*

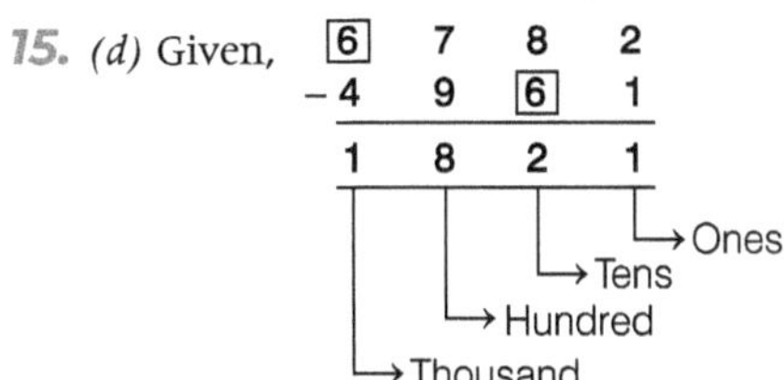

Jack cycled from B to C = 479 m
Then, he cycled from C to A = 479 + 362 = 841 m
Total distance covered by Jack
 = Distance from B to C + Distance from C to A
 = 841 + 479 = 1320 m

15. *(d)* Given,

$$\begin{array}{cccc} \boxed{6} & 7 & 8 & 2 \\ -\,4 & 9 & \boxed{6} & 1 \\ \hline 1 & 8 & 2 & 1 \end{array}$$

→ Ones
→ Tens
→ Hundred
→ Thousand

$A = 6$, $B = 6$
Hence, $A - B = 6 - 6 = 0$

16. *(c)* $A = 3247 + 4653 = 7900$
$B = 6253 - 4132 = 2121$
$C = 2417 + 6215 = 8632$
$D = 8356 - 3421 = 4935$
Now, according to the question, $(A + D) - (B + C)$
 $= (7900 + 4935) - (2121 + 8632)$
 $= 12835 - 10753 = 2082$

17. *(d)* We have, $\bigcirc + \triangle = 30$

$\triangle + \triangle = 40$

and $\triangle + \square = 50$

So, we get $2 \times \triangle = 40$
[as multiplication is repreated addition]
So, $\triangle = 40 \div 2 = 20$
Now, $\bigcirc + \triangle = 30$
So, $\bigcirc = 30 - \triangle$
 $= 30 - 20 = 10$
Also, $\triangle + \square = 50$
So, $\square = 50 - \triangle$
 $= 50 - 20 = 30$
Therefore, $\bigcirc + \square = 10 + 30$
i.e., ✿ $= 40$
So, option (d) is correct.

18. *(b)* Water contained by fish tank already
 $= 490$ mL
Water poured in a fish tank = 630 mL
and water spilled out from tank = 120 mL

so, the volume of water in the fish tank finally =
Initially water in fish tank
 + water poured in fish tank
 − water spilled out.
 $= 490 + 630 - 120 = 1120 - 120 = 1000$ mL

19. *(b)* Given number is

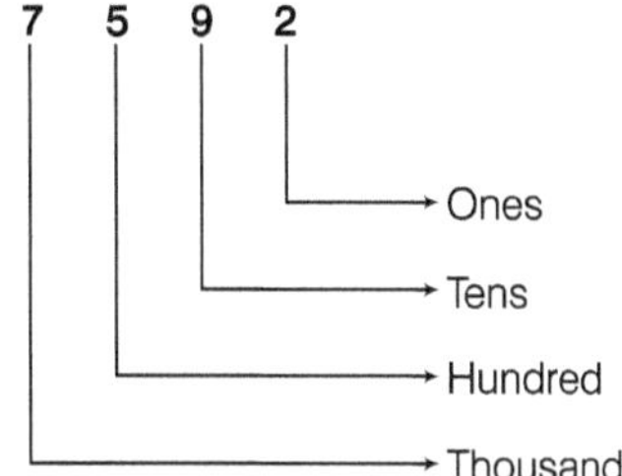

$$\begin{array}{cccc} 7 & 5 & 9 & 2 \end{array}$$

→ Ones
→ Tens
→ Hundred
→ Thousand

So, place value of 7 in 7592 = $7 \times 1000 = 7000$
and place value of 2 in 7592 = $2 \times 1 = 2$
∴ Difference of the place value of 7 and 2
 in 7592 = $7000 - 2 = 6998$

20. *(d)* Number of stamps Aslam has = 324
So, Number of stamps Ravi has
 = Number of stamps Aslam has − 124
 = $324 - 124 = 200$

Chapter 3 :
Multiplication and Division

1. *(b)* Number of * in each rectangle = 6
Number of rectangles = 4
So, total number of * = $6 \times 4 = 24$

2. *(a)* In row 1, the 15 counters are divided in 5
groups having three counters each.
So, row 1 represents $5 \times 3 = 15$
In row 2, the 15 counters are divided in 3 groups
having 5 counters each.
So, row 2 represents $3 \times 5 = 15$
Therefore, we get the representation as
 $5 \times 3 = 15 = 3 \times 5$
i.e., $5 \times 3 = 3 \times 5$

3. *(d)* Number of colours in a rainbow = 7
Number of sets of cupcake for each colour = 7
and number of cupcakes in each set = 6
So, total number of cupcakes Samantha made
 = Number of colours in rainbow × Number of
 sets for each colour × Number of cupcakes
 in each set
 $= 7 \times 7 \times 6 = 294$

4. *(a)* In a report, each line has 21 words.
Total lines in a report is 62.

So, total number of words in a report
= word in each line × total number of lines
= 21 × 62 = 1302

5. *(a)* Number of students in Jolly's class
= Number of students in 1 row × Number of students in 1 column = 15 × 5 = 75
Amount of money contributed by each student = ₹ 3
So, total amount of money collected
= Number of students × Money contributed by each student = 75 × 3 = ₹ 225
So, option (a) is correct.

6. *(c)* One Japamala contains 108 beads.
So, number of beads in 15 Japamala
= Number of Japamala
× beads containing each Japamala
= 15 × 108 = 1620

7. *(d)* Number of bird houses built in a day = 5
Number of bird houses built in 7 days
(1 week) = 7 × 5
Number of bird houses broken by the dog = 2
So, number of bird houses left unbroken
= (7 × 5) − 2

8. *(d)* Number of pencils Suzene has = 80
Number of friends to whom Suzene gave these pencils = 10
So, number of pencils each friend got = 80 ÷ 10

9. *(b)* Number of stamps in collection A = 17 (odd)
Number of stamps in collection B = 18 (even)
Number of stamps in collection C = 25 (odd)
Number of stamps in collection D = 19 (odd)
Eric can share the stamps equally, if the number of stamps is divisible by 2.
We see that the number of stamps in collection B is an even number
i.e., divisible by 2.
Hence, Eric can share the stamps in collection *B* equally with his sister.

10. *(c)* Number of pens Marshall had = Δ
Number of pens Ann had = 14
Product of the number of pens Ann and Marshall have = 56
i.e.,   Δ × 14 = 56
So, number of pens Marshall had = 56 ÷ 14
∴   Δ = 56 ÷ 14
Hence, option (c) is correct.

11. *(a)* Let the other number be *x*.
According to the question,
$$x \times a = 2979$$
⇒ $x = 2979 \div 9 \Rightarrow x = 331$
so, the difference = 331 − 9 = 322

12. *(d)* Number of shelves to keep apples in the shop = 4
Number of apples that can be kept in one shelf = 15
So, total number of apples that can be kept in 4 shelves = 15 × 4 = 60
Now, number of apples Ms. Bendick has = 72
So, number of apples that will not be able to fit in the shelf = 72 − 60 = 12

13. *(c)* The distance of the place = 300 miles
So, half of the distance = 300 ÷ 2 = 150 miles
Point, where they stopped for lunch = 10 miles before the half point = 150 − 10 = 140 miles
So, distance they still have to travel to reach the destination = 300 − 140 = 160 miles

14. *(a)* As we know,
Dividend = Divisor × Quotient + Remainder
According to the question,
Dividend = 489
Divisor = 7
Remainder = 6
Quotient = □
We put these values in above formula,
$$489 = 7 \times □ + 6$$
⇒ $489 − 6 = 7 \times □$
⇒ $483 = 7 \times □$
⇒ $□ = 483 \div 7$
∴   Quotient = 69

15. *(a)* (a) Incorrect,
$115 \div 5 = 23, 115 \times 0 = 0$
23 is greater than 0.
(b) Correct,
$480 \div 6 = 80, 16 \times 5 = 80$
So, $480 \div 6 = 16 \times 5$
(c) Correct,
$12 \times 5 = 60, 12 + 12 + 12 + 12 + 12 = 60$
(d) Correct,
$65 \times 1 = 65, 1 \times 65 = 65$
Hence, option (a) is incorrect

16. *(d)* 1. False,
$2 \times 7 = 14$ and $7 \times 7 = 49$
So, they are not equal.
2. False,
$8 \div 4 = 2$ and $8 + 8 + 8 + 8 = 32$
So, they are not equal.
3. True,
$44 \div A = B + 1$
If $A = 4$ and $B = 10$, then
$44 \div 4 = 11$
and $10 + 1 = 11$

4. True,

    e.g. 30, 140, 1260 all are divisible by 10.

17. *(b)* Amount of money saved by Ronit daily

$$= ₹1.25$$

Number of days in a month of June

$$= 30$$

Total money saved in month of June

$$= 30 \times ₹\, 1.25 = ₹\, 37.5$$

18. *(a)* (A) 1 pair socks have 2 socks, then
12 pairs = 24 socks, correct.

    (B) 1 Rainbow has 7 colour, then 5 rainbow has

$$= 7 \times 5 = 35, \text{ correct.}$$

    (C) 1 dice has 6 face, then 8 dice = $8 \times 6 = 48$,
incorrect.

    (D) Chess has 64 total boxes, 32 white and
32 black, correct.

    Hence, (C) statement is incorrect.

19. *(c)* Money paid by Linda's uncle and aunt to
mow their yard = ₹ 12 each week

Money paid by Linda's uncle and aunt to wash
their dog = ₹ 2 each week.

Number of weeks worked by Linda = 7

So, total money paid for mowing the yard

$$= 12 \times 7$$

and total money paid for washing the dog

$$= 2 \times 7$$

∴ Total money paid for both the works

$$= (12 \times 7) + (2 \times 7)$$

So, option (c) is correct.

20. *(b)* We can clearly observe that,

$$7\ \boxed{2}\ 9$$
$$\underline{\times\ 6}$$
$$43\ \boxed{7}\ 4$$

    $P = 2, Q = 7$

Hence, $P + Q = 2 + 7 = 9$

So, option (b) is correct.

Chapter 4 : Fractions

1. *(c)* Total number of parts in the figure = 8

      Number of parts shaded = 5

So, fraction showing the number of shaded

$$\text{parts} = \frac{\text{Number of shaded parts}}{\text{Total number of parts}} = \frac{5}{8}$$

2. *(b)* In option (b), fraction of shaded parts $= \dfrac{2}{3}$

In option (b), fraction of shaded parts $= \dfrac{6}{10}$

In option (c), fraction of shaded parts $= \dfrac{4}{7}$

In option (d), fraction of shaded parts $= \dfrac{4}{6}$

In options (a), (c) and (d), fraction of shaded
parts does not show a correct fraction.

So, option (b) is correct.

3. *(a)* There are $\underline{7}$ tenths are present in the fraction
$\dfrac{7}{10}$.

4. *(a)* Considering following option

From figure in option (a) : $\dfrac{1}{5} < \dfrac{3}{5}$

From figure in option (b) : $\dfrac{1}{4} < \dfrac{2}{4}$

From figure in option (c) : $\dfrac{1}{3} = \dfrac{1}{3}$

From figure in option (d) : $\dfrac{2}{4} > \dfrac{4}{10}$

So, figure sets in option (a) shows the $\dfrac{1}{5} < \dfrac{3}{5}$.

Hence, option (a) is correct.

5. *(c)* Number of days of which weather forecast is
given = 5

Number of sunny days = 3

So, fraction of sunny days

$$= \frac{\text{Number of sunny days}}{\text{Total number of days}} = \frac{3}{5}$$

6. *(c)* Equivalent fraction of $\dfrac{1}{3}$ with numerator 7 is

$$\frac{1}{3} \times \frac{7}{7} = \frac{7}{21}$$

7. *(d)* In the word 'NUMERATOR',

Total number of letters = 9

Number of letters made up of more than three
straight lines = 2 (M, E)

So, fraction of alphabets made up of more than

three straight lines

$$= \frac{\begin{array}{c}\text{Number of letters made up of three}\\ \text{straight lines}\end{array}}{\text{Total number of letters}} = \frac{2}{9}$$

8. *(d)* Number of stickers Jady has $= 17$

Number of stickers given to Amantha = 4
and number of stickers given to Ruby = 6

Total number of stickers given $= 4 + 6 = 10$

Number of stickers left

$$= \text{Total number of stickers}$$
$$- \text{Number of stickers given}$$
$$= 17 - 10 = 7$$

So, Fraction of stickers left

$$= \frac{\text{Number of stickers left}}{\text{Total number of stickers}} = \frac{7}{17}$$

9. *(b)* Number of cupcakes Kristane bought = 30

Number of cupcakes eaten by her = 6

So, number of cupcakes left = 30 − 6 = 24

Now, number of cupcakes given to her sister

$$= \frac{3}{4} \text{ of remaining cupcakes}$$

$$= \frac{3}{4} \times 24 = \frac{72}{4} = 18$$

So, number of cupcakes now left with Kristane

$$= 24 - 18 = 6$$

∴ Fraction of cupcakes left with Kristane $= \dfrac{6}{30}$

10. *(c)* Fraction of money spent on buying vegetables $= \dfrac{1}{4}$

Fraction of money spent on buying fruits $= \dfrac{1}{2}$

Fraction of money spent on buying grocery products $= \dfrac{1}{4}$

Now, figure in option (c) represents

Vegetables $\frac{1}{4}$	Fruits $\frac{1}{2}$
Grocery products $\frac{1}{4}$	

So, option (c) is correct.

11. *(a)*

1. True, the triangle is divided into three equal parts.

2. True,

   Fraction of shaded part in ⬚ $= \dfrac{1}{4}$

   and fraction of shaded part in ⬚ $= \dfrac{1}{5}$

   and $\dfrac{1}{4} > \dfrac{1}{5}$.

3. False, $\dfrac{7}{7} = 1$, so it represents the whole.

12. *(d)* 1. $\dfrac{5}{8}$

   Total number of stars = 8

   Number of shaded stars = 5

   So, fraction of shaded stars $= \dfrac{5}{8}$

   2. $\dfrac{1}{2}$

   Number of trees = 8

Number of encircled trees = 4

So, fraction of encircled trees $= \dfrac{4}{8} = \dfrac{1}{2}$

3. $\dfrac{3}{8}$

Number of letters in the word 'FRACTION' = 8

Number of vowels = 3 (A, I, O)

So, fraction of vowels $= \dfrac{3}{8}$

4. $1\dfrac{1}{4}$

If ⬤ = 1, then

⬤ ⊕ $= 1 + \dfrac{1}{4} = 1\dfrac{1}{4}$

So, 1 → C, 2 → D, 3 → F, 4 → B.

Hence, option (d) is correct.

13. *(b)* Number of cards made by Zoya = 5

Number of cards made by Jeniffer = 1

Number of cards made by Dany = 2

Number of cards made by Linda = 0

So, total number of cards made

$$= 5 + 1 + 2 + 0 = 8$$

So, fraction of cards made by Zoya $= \dfrac{5}{8}$

Fraction of cards made by Jeniffer $= \dfrac{1}{8}$

Fraction of cards made by Dany $= \dfrac{2}{8}$

Fraction of cards made by Linda $= \dfrac{0}{8} = 0$

∴ A → 3, B → 2, C → 1, D → 4

Hence, option (b) is correct.

14. *(a)* Number of handkerchieves bought by Rachel's mother = 45

Number of handkerchieves used by Rachel each day = 2

So, number of handkerchieves used by Rachel in 10 days = 10 × 2 = 20

Number of handkerchives not used by her in 10 days = 45 − 20 = 25

So, fraction of handkerchieves not used by Rachel in 10 days $= \dfrac{25}{45}$

15. *(d)* As we know, when the denominator of fractions are same, then fraction with the greatest numerator is greater and vice-versa.

So, the correct descending order is

$$\frac{11}{4} > \frac{9}{4} > \frac{7}{4} > \frac{5}{4}$$

Hence, option (d) is correct.

16. *(c)* As we know, when the numerators of fractions are same, then the fraction with the greatest denominator is smaller and *vice-versa*.
So, the correct ascending order is
$$\frac{3}{12} < \frac{3}{9} < \frac{3}{8} < \frac{3}{7}$$
$\therefore \dfrac{3}{8}$ is the second greatest fraction.

17. *(b)* According to the question,
$$\frac{7}{10} - \frac{4}{10} = \frac{A}{B} = \frac{3}{10}$$
$$\frac{3}{15} + \frac{8}{15} = \frac{C}{D} = \frac{11}{15}$$
$\therefore A = 3, B = 10, C = 11, D = 15$
$\therefore (B - A) + (D - C) = (10 - 3) + (15 - 11) = 7 + 4 = 11$

18. *(b)* According to the question,
$$\frac{1}{9} + \frac{4}{9} - \frac{2}{9} = \frac{3}{9}$$
and
$$\frac{5}{9} + \frac{2}{9} - \frac{3}{9} = \frac{4}{9}$$
Now, we know when denominator is same, then the fraction with greater numerator is greater.
So, $\dfrac{1}{9} + \dfrac{4}{9} - \dfrac{2}{9} \boxed{<} \dfrac{5}{9} + \dfrac{2}{9} - \dfrac{3}{9}$

19. *(b)* (P) $\dfrac{5}{9} - \dfrac{4}{9} = \dfrac{5-4}{9} = \dfrac{1}{9}$

(Q) $\dfrac{2}{4} + \dfrac{1}{4} + \dfrac{3}{4} = \dfrac{2+1+3}{4} = \dfrac{6}{4}$

(R) $\dfrac{2}{11} + \dfrac{9}{11} - \dfrac{4}{11} = \dfrac{2+9}{11} - \dfrac{4}{11}$
$= \dfrac{11}{11} - \dfrac{4}{11} = \dfrac{11-4}{11} = \dfrac{7}{11}$

(S) $\dfrac{14}{19} - \dfrac{6}{19} = \dfrac{14-6}{19} = \dfrac{8}{19}$

So, P-(ii); Q-(iv); R-(i); S-(iii).
Hence, option (b) is correct.

20. *(d)* Numbers having odd digit at the tens place
= 276, 432, 892, 214, 96
Total numbers written = 11
So, fraction of numbers having odd digit at the tens place
$$= \frac{\text{Number of numbers having odd digit at tens place}}{\text{Total number of numbers}} = \frac{5}{11}$$

21. *(b)* Fraction showing number of each musical instrument

Drums $= \dfrac{6}{12}$

Guitar $= \dfrac{2}{12}$

Flute $= \dfrac{3}{12}$

Violin $= \dfrac{1}{12}$

Total number of guitars Deborah has
$$= \frac{2}{12} \times 24 = 4$$

22. *(b)* Total number of flutes Deborah has
$$= \frac{3}{12} \times 24 = 6$$
Fraction of flutes Deborah gave to her brother
$$= \frac{1}{3}$$
So, number of flutes she gave to her brother
$$= \frac{1}{3} \times 6 = 2$$
$\therefore$ Number of flutes she is left with $= 6 - 2 = 4$

23. *(c)* According to the question,

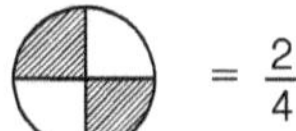 $= \dfrac{1}{4}$

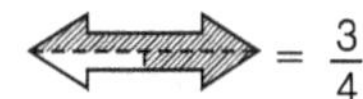 $= \dfrac{2}{4}$

$= \dfrac{3}{4}$

$\therefore$ Sum of fractions $= \dfrac{1}{4} + \dfrac{2}{4} + \dfrac{3}{4} = \dfrac{1+2+3}{4} = \dfrac{6}{4}$

24. *(c)* Total number of students = 20
Number of students who like juice and not milkshake = 6 + 5 = 11
Fraction of students who like juice and not milkshake $= \dfrac{11}{20}$.

Chapter 5 : Measurements

1. *(c)* Observe the scale carefully, the height of elephant is 38 cm.

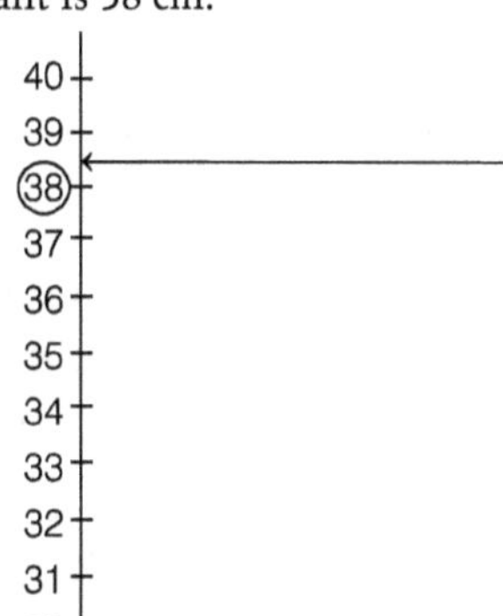

Hence, option (c) is correct.

2. *(b)* The length of the pencil starts from 20 cm and ends at 36 cm.
So, the length of the pencil
$$= 36 \text{ cm} - 20 \text{ cm} = 16 \text{ cm}$$
The length of the pen starts from 16 cm and ends at 31 cm.
So, the length of the pen
$$= 31 \text{ cm} - 16 \text{ cm} = 15 \text{ cm}$$
So, the pencil is longer than pen.

3. *(c)* Length of one safety pin $= 3$ cm
Length of seven safety pins $= (7 \times 3)$ cm $= 21$ cm
So, length of hairbursh $= 21$ cm
[as given seven safety pins can cover the length of hairbrush]

4. *(d)* Thermometer in option (d) shows 77°F.
Hence, option (d) is correct.

5. *(d)* Given, temperature shown in the thermometer is 25°F more than room temperature.
According to the question,
$$40° \text{ F} = 25° \text{ F} + \text{Room temperature}$$
So, room temperature $= 40° \text{ F} - 25° \text{ F} = 15° \text{ F}$

6. *(c)* Distance travelled in each option is
(a) School $\xrightarrow{2 \text{ km}}$ Bank $\xrightarrow{1 \text{ km}}$ Market $\xrightarrow{3 \text{ km}}$ House
$$= 2 \text{ km} + 1 \text{ km} + 3 \text{ km} = 6 \text{ km}$$
(b) School $\xrightarrow{2 \text{ km}}$ Bank $\xrightarrow{3 \text{ km}}$ House
$$= 2 \text{ km} + 3 \text{ km} = 5 \text{ km}$$
(c) School $\xrightarrow{3 \text{ km}}$ Playground $\xrightarrow{1 \text{ km}}$ House
$$= 3 \text{ km} + 1 \text{ km} = 4 \text{ km}$$
Since, 4 km is the shortest distance.
So, option (c) is correct.

7. *(a)* One who cover the shortest distance will reach the playground first.
(Distance for Raghav to reach playground)
$$= 113 \text{ m} + 171 \text{ m} = 284 \text{ m}$$
Distance for Mehul to reach Playground
$$= 100 \text{ m} + 190 \text{ m} = 290 \text{ m}$$
So, Raghav will reach first to play ground.

8. *(c)* The weight shown by each weighing scale is
Option (a), 150 g
Option (b), 330 g
Option (c), 320 g
Option (d), 450 g
So, weighing machine in option (c) shows the correct weight.

9. *(c)* Weight of bag
$$= 1 \text{ kg} + \frac{1}{2} \text{ kg} + 1 \text{ kg} + 1 \text{ kg}$$
$$= 1000 \text{ g} + 500 \text{ g} + 1000 \text{ g} + 1000 \text{ g} = 3500 \text{ g}$$
$$\left[\begin{array}{l} \because \quad 1 \text{ kg} = 1000 \text{ g} \\ \text{and} \frac{1}{2} \text{ kg} = 500 \text{ g} \end{array} \right]$$

10. *(b)* Weight of tomatoes bought
$$= 2550 \text{ g} = 2000 \text{ g} + 550 \text{ g}$$
$$= 2 \text{ kg } 550 \text{ g} \qquad [\because 1 \text{ kg} = 1000 \text{ g}]$$
Total weight in each option is
(a) 1 kg + 500 g + 200 g + 200 g + 200 g + 250 g
$$= 2350 \text{ g} = 2 \text{ kg } 350 \text{ g}$$
(b) 1 kg + 500 g + 250 g + 250 g + 200 g + 200 g + 100 g + 50 g
$$= 2550 \text{ g} = 2 \text{ kg } 550 \text{ g}$$
(c) 500 g + 500 g + 500 g + 250 g + 250 g + 200 g + 50 g
$$= 2250 \text{ g} = 2 \text{ kg } 250 \text{ g}$$
So, option (b) is correct.

11. *(b)* Weight of fruits bought from shop A
$$= 2 \text{ kg } 563 \text{ g} = 2000 \text{ g} + 563 \text{ g}$$
$$= 2563 \text{ g} \qquad [\because 1 \text{ kg} = 1000 \text{ g}]$$
Weight of fruits bought from shop B
$$= 1 \text{ kg } 839 \text{ g}$$
$$= 1000 \text{ g} + 839 \text{ g} \qquad [\because 1 \text{ kg} = 1000 \text{ g}]$$
$$= 1839 \text{ g}$$
More quantity of fruits bought from shop A than from shop B
$$= 2563 \text{ g} - 1839 \text{ g} = 724 \text{ g}$$

12. *(b)* Weight of Shelly $= 25$ kg
Weight of Jeniffer $=$ Weight of Shelly $- 5$ kg
$$= 25 \text{ kg} - 5 \text{ kg} = 20 \text{ kg}$$
Weight of Maria $=$ Weight of Shelly $+ 12$ kg
$$= 25 \text{ kg} + 12 \text{ kg} = 37 \text{ kg}$$
So, total weight of all three
$$= 25 \text{ kg} + 20 \text{ kg} + 37 \text{ kg} = 82 \text{ kg}$$

13. *(a)* Quantity of orange juice poured
$$= 725 \text{ mL}$$
Quantity of pineapple juice poured
$$= 845 \text{ mL}$$
Quantity of cranberry juice poured
$$= 965 \text{ mL}$$
So, total quantity of juice poured in the jug
$$= 725 \text{ mL} + 845 \text{ mL} + 965 \text{ mL}$$
$$= 2535 \text{ mL}$$
$$= 2 \text{ L } 535 \text{ mL} \quad [\because 1 \text{ L} = 1000 \text{ mL}]$$

14. *(c)* Quantity of water a bucket can hold
$$= 2L = 2000 \text{ mL} \quad [\because 1 \text{ L} = 1000 \text{ mL}]$$
Quantity of water in each option is
(a) 200 mL + 200 mL + 250 mL + 250 mL
$$+ \: 500 \text{ mL} = 1400 \text{ mL}$$
(b) 250 mL + 250 mL + 500 mL + 500 mL
$$+ \: 300 \text{ mL} = 1800 \text{ mL}$$
(c) 500 mL + 250 mL + 250 mL + 250 mL
$$+ \: 250 \text{ mL} + 500 \text{ mL} = 2000 \text{ mL}$$
So, option (c) is correct.

15. *(d)* Number of milk packets Richard has = 6

Number of milk packet fell on the floor = 1
Now, number of milk packets left = 6 − 1 = 5
Given, capacity of 1 packet
$$= 3 \text{ L } 35 \text{ mL} = 3035 \text{ mL}$$
∴ Quantity of milk left with Richard
$$= 3035 \times 5 = 15175 \text{ mL}$$
So, 15175 mL = 15 L 175 mL $[\because 1 \text{ L} = 1000 \text{ mL}]$

16. *(c)* Capacity of oil-can bought = 7 L = 7000 mL
$$[\because 1 \text{ L} = 1000 \text{ mL}]$$
Capacity of beaker used = 700 mL
So, the number of times the beaker can be filled
by the oil
$$= \frac{\text{Capacity of oil-can}}{\text{Capacity of beaker}} = \frac{7000 \text{ mL}}{700 \text{ mL}} = 10$$

17. *(d)* Capacity of jug = 2 L

Capacity of jug when it is half = 1 L
Pouring 5 full mugs is equal to half jug.
5 full mug = 1 L
1 full mug = 1000 mL ÷ 5 $[\because 1 \text{ L} = 1000 \text{ mL}]$
$$= 200 \text{ mL}$$
So, capacity of mug, when it is half
$$= 200 \text{ mL} \div 2 = 100 \text{ mL}$$

18. *(d)* Distance between John's home and mall
= 150 m
∴ Distance between mall and bank
$$= 150 \times 2 = 300 \text{ m}$$

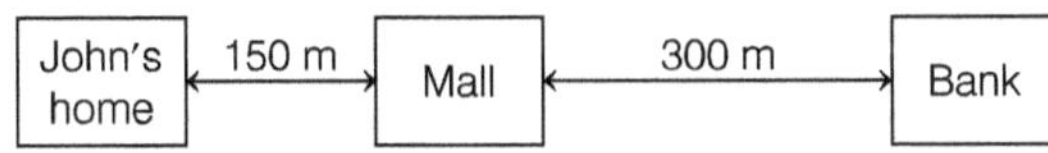

(a) Distance between John's home to bank and
back to home
$$= 150 + 300 + 450 = 900 \text{ m}$$
(b) Distance covered by John from mall to bank
and back to his home
= Distance between mall and bank
$$+ \text{ Distance between bank and}$$
$$\text{John's home}$$
$$= 300 + 450 = 750 \text{ m}$$

19. *(a)* Given, weight of one △ = 250 g

Then, weight of 6△ = 250 gm × 6 = 1500 g
As, weight of 4 □ = weight of 6 △
⇒ Weight of 4 □ = 1500 g
Weight of 1 □ = 1500 ÷ 4 = 375 g

20. *(b)* 1. 38 cm

Total length of ribbon = 266 cm
So, length of each part = 266 ÷ 7 = 38 cm
2. 150 g
Total sugar bought = 746 g
Sugar used = 596 g
So, amount of sugar left
$$= 746 \text{ g} - 596 \text{ g}$$
$$= 150 \text{ g}$$
3. 700 mL
Total amount of lemonade
$$= 250 \text{ ml} + 450 \text{ ml}$$
$$= 700 \text{ ml}$$
4. 7 kg
Total quantity of vegetables bought
$$= 1046 \text{ g} + 5954 \text{ g}$$
$$= 7000 \text{ g} = 7 \text{ kg} \qquad [\because 1 \text{ kg} = 1000 \text{ g}]$$
So, 1 → F,   2 → G,   3 → E,   4 → B.
Hence, option (b) is correct.

Chapter 6 : Money

1. *(c)* Amount of money Michelle has = ₹ 452

We know,   ₹ 1 = 100 paise
So,   ₹ 452 = 452 × 100 paise
$$= 45200 \text{ paise}$$

2. *(a)* Amount of money Braden has
= Five hundred forty six rupees fifty paise
= Rupees → 546 and paise → 50 = ₹ 546.50
Given, price of 1 kg apples = ₹ 527.40
$$[\: 527.40 < 546.50]$$
Price of 1 kg mangos = ₹ 572.00
$$[\: 572 > 546.50]$$
Price of 1 kg guavas = ₹ 556.75
$$[\: 556.75 > 546.50]$$
So, Braden can buy 1 kg apples.

3. *(a)* Cost of pair of shoes = ₹ 1500

Amount of money left
$$= \text{Thirty five thousand paise}$$
$$= 35000 \text{ paise}$$
$$= ₹ 350 \qquad [\because ₹ 1 = 100 \text{ paise}]$$
So, total money Sandy had
$$= ₹ 1500 + ₹ 350$$

4. *(c)* Number of 5 rupees coins = 2
Number of 2 rupees coins = 2
Number of 1 rupee coins = 2
Number of 50 paise coins = 2
Number of 25 paise coins = 1
Number of 10 paise coins = 1
Combination of coins that can sum of ₹ 6.25.
1. ₹ 5 + ₹ 1 + ₹ 0.25 = ₹ 6.25
2. ₹ 5 + ₹ 0.50 + ₹ 0.50 + ₹ 0.25 = ₹ 6.25
3. ₹ 2 + ₹ 2 + ₹ 1 + ₹ 1 + ₹ 0.25 = ₹ 6.25
4. ₹ 2 + ₹ 2 + ₹ 1 + ₹ 0.50 + ₹ 0.50 + ₹ 0.25 = ₹ 6.25
So, four combinations can be formed.

5. *(c)* Amount of money Anjali has
$$= 12 \text{ rupees } 60 \text{ paise}$$
$$= 1200 \text{ paise} + 60 \text{ paise}$$
$$[\because ₹ 1 = 100 \text{ paise}]$$
$$= 1260 \text{ paise} = ₹ 1260$$
Cost of notebook = 9 rupees 50 paise
$$= 900 \text{ paise} + 50 \text{ paise}$$
$$= 950 \text{ paise} = ₹ 9.50$$
So, amount of money Anjali will get back
$$= ₹ 1260 - ₹ 9.50$$
$$= 1260 \text{ paise} - 950 \text{ paise} = 310 \text{ paise}$$

6. *(d)* Total money Tyran has = ₹ 400.25
Money paid for ticket = ₹ 180.75
Cost of sandwich he bought = ₹ 40.50
Cost of soft drink he bought = ₹ 25.00
Total money spent
$$= ₹ 180.75 + ₹ 40.50 + ₹ 25.00 = ₹ 246.25$$
So, amount of money left with Tyran
= Total amount he had – Amount of money
he spent
$$= ₹ 400.25 - ₹ 246.25 = ₹ 154$$

7. *(b)* Given, Zara has = ₹ 350
Amount of different toy in each option is
(a) Cost of 1 toy bike + Cost of 1 toy
submarine
$$= ₹ 210.25 + ₹ 375.50 = ₹ 585.75$$
(b) Cost of 1 dancing doll = ₹ 308.75
(c) Cost of 1 sea animal sticker + 1 toy bike
$$= ₹ 175 + ₹ 210.25$$
$$= ₹ 385.25$$
(d) Cost of 1 toy submarine = ₹ 375.50
So, Zara can buy only dancing doll.
Hence, option (b) is correct.

8. *(a)* Given, cost of 1 toy submarine = ₹ 375.50
and cost of 1 toy bike = ₹ 210.25
So, Zack will get money back
$$= ₹ 375.50 - ₹ 210.25$$
$$= ₹ 165.25$$

9. *(d)* A. ₹ 5.50 + 25 paisa = ₹ 5.75
B. ₹ 5.25 – 50 paisa = ₹ 5.25
C. ₹ 5.25 + 75 paisa = ₹ 6
D. ₹ 5.75 + 10 paisa = ₹ 5.85
E. ₹ 5.90 – 10 paisa = ₹ 5.80
So, A → 2; B → 1; C → 3; D → 5; E → 4;
Hence, option (d) is correct.

10. *(c)* Total amount of money spent by Rohit
$$= ₹ 500 + ₹ 100 + ₹ 20 + ₹ 10 + ₹ 10 + ₹ 10$$
$$+ ₹ 5 + ₹ 2 + ₹ 1 + ₹ 1$$
$$= ₹ 659$$
Amount of money Rohit had in the beginning
$$= ₹ 2000$$
So, amount of money left with him
$$= ₹ 2000 - ₹ 659 = ₹ 1341$$

11. *(c)* Total money = ₹ 100 + ₹ 50 + ₹ 20 + 10 + ₹ 5
$$+ ₹ 2 = ₹ 187$$

12. *(d)* Total money = ₹ 187 to be divided equally
among 5
Each boy will bet = 187 ÷ 5 = ₹ 37.40

13. *(b)* Given, cost of one sticker = 35 paise
∴ Cost of six stickers = (35 × 6) paise
$$= 210 \text{ paise}$$
$$= 200 \text{ paise} + 10 \text{ paise}$$
$$= ₹ 2 + 10 \text{ paise}$$
$$[\because ₹ 1 = 100 \text{ paise}]$$
$$= 2 \text{ rupees } 10 \text{ paise}$$

14. *(c)* 1. True, Indian unit of money is rupee.
2. False, symbol for paise is P.
3. False, 1 rupee = 100 paise
4. True,
Given, cost of 1 stamp = 15 paise
So, cost of 40 stamps = (40 × 15) paise
$$= 600 \text{ paise}$$
$$= ₹ 6 \quad [\because ₹ 1 = 100 \text{ paise}]$$

15. *(b)* 1. ₹ 2.70
Total value to be added
$$= 2 × 0.10 + 2 × 0.25 + 2 × 0.50 + ₹ 1$$
$$= ₹ 0.20 + ₹ 0.50 + ₹ 1 + ₹ 1$$
$$\begin{bmatrix} \because \ 2 × 0.10 = 0.10 + 0.10 = ₹ 0.20 \\ 2 × 0.25 = 0.25 + 0.25 = ₹ 0.50 \\ \text{and } 2 × 0.50 = 0.50 + 0.50 = ₹ 1 \end{bmatrix}$$
$$= ₹ 2.70$$
2. 15 paise
$$\Rightarrow \ ? = ₹ 1 - (10 \text{ paise} + 25 \text{ paise} + 50 \text{ paise})$$
$$= 100 \text{ paise} - 85 \text{ paise}$$
$$[\because ₹ 1 = 100 \text{ paise}]$$
$$= 15 \text{ paise}$$

3. ₹ 1.75
   $\Rightarrow$ 1 rupee 75 paise = ₹ 1.75
4. 50 paise,
   $\Rightarrow$ 5×10 paise = 50 paise
∴ $1 \rightarrow$ G, $2 \rightarrow$ D, $3 \rightarrow$ B, $4 \rightarrow$ E
Hence, option (b) is correct.

16. *(d)* Money earned by John in a month
   = ₹ 560
Amount of money spend by him in a month
   = ₹ 440
Money save by him in a month
   = ₹ 560 − ₹ 440 = ₹ 120
So, amount of money save in a year
   = ₹ (120×12)
         [∵ 1 year = 12 months]
   = ₹ 1440

17. *(d)* Cost of 1 ticket for adult
   = Forty six rupees and seventy five paise
Rupees $\rightarrow$ 46, paise $\rightarrow$ 75 = ₹ 46.75
Cost of 1 ticket for child = Nineteen rupees an
                     seventy five paise
Rupees $\rightarrow$ 19, paise $\rightarrow$ 75 = ₹ 19.75
Cost of tickets for 16 children
   = $16 \times$ ₹ 19.75 = ₹ 316
So, total cost of tickets
   = ₹ 46.75 + ₹ 316 = ₹ 362.75

18. *(a)* We have,
3 pencils + 1 sharpener = ₹ 5   ...(i)
2 sharpeners + 2 erasers = ₹ 8   ...(ii)
3 erasers = ₹ 6
Then, 1 eraser = ₹ 6 ÷ 3 = ₹ 2
         So, 2 sharpeners + $2 \times$ ₹ 2 = ₹ 8
                     [from above]
$\Rightarrow$ 2 sharpeners + ₹ 4 = ₹ 8
$\Rightarrow$ 2 sharpeners = ₹ 8 − ₹ 4
$\Rightarrow$ 2 sharpeners = ₹ 4
So,   1 sharpener = ₹ 4 ÷ 2 = ₹ 2
Now, consider 3 pencils + 1 sharpener = ₹ 5
$\Rightarrow$ 3 pencils + ₹ 2 = ₹ 5 [from above]
$\Rightarrow$ 3 pencils = ₹ 5 − ₹ 2 = ₹ 3
So,   1 pencil = ₹ 3 ÷ 3 = ₹ 1
Thus, the cost of one pencil is ₹ 1.

19. *(b)* Given, cost of video game = ₹ 750
Money saved by Jack every week = 2500 paise
         = ₹ 25   [∵ ₹ 1 = 100 paise]
So, number of weeks in which ₹ 750 will be
saved = Total money to be saved
         ÷ Money saved in one week
   = ₹ 750 ÷ ₹ 25 = 30

20. *(c)* Given, amount of money George has = ₹ 1200
Cost of 1 jeans = ₹ 675
Cost of 1 bag = ₹ 725
Cost of 1 T-shirt = ₹ 525
Cost of 1 watch = ₹ 550
Consider, Cost of 1 bag + 1 jeans
         = ₹ 725 + ₹ 675 = ₹ 1400
Cost of 1 watch + 1 T-shirt = ₹ 550 + ₹ 525
         = ₹ 1075
Cost of 1 jeans + 1 T-shirt = ₹ 675 + ₹ 525 = ₹ 1200
Cost of 1 bag + 1 watch = ₹ 725 + ₹ 550 = ₹ 1275
So, George can buy a jeans and a T-shirt in the
amount of money he had.
Hence, option (c) is correct.

21. *(a)* Money in Jinnie's piggy bank = ₹ 133
Money gave by her grandparents = ₹ 16
Money added by Jinnie in 1 week
         = 12 rupees 50 paise = ₹ 1250
Money added by Jinnie in 6 weeks
         = ₹ 1250 × 6 = ₹ 75
So, total money saved in 6 weeks
         = ₹ 133 + ₹ 16 + ₹ 75 = ₹ 224
         = ₹ 200 + 20 + 4 [expanded form]
         = ₹ 2 hundred 2 tens 4 ones

22. *(b)* Total of bill A = ₹ 20.75 + ₹ 35.50 + ₹ 50.25
         = ₹ 106.5
Total of bill B = ₹ 20.25 + ₹ 30.75 + ₹ 15.00 = ₹ 66
Total of bill C = ₹ 40.45 + ₹ 13.15 + ₹ 75.00
         = ₹ 128.6
Total of bill D = ₹ 60.50 + ₹ 30.00 + ₹ 20.50
         = ₹ 111
So, bill C has the highest amount.

23. *(c)* Cost of 1 pack of pencils
         = 10 rupees 50 paise = ₹ 10.50
Cost of 1 pack of pens = 15 rupees 25 paise
         = ₹ 15.25
For Carol,
Cost of 1 pack of pencils + 4 packs of pens
         = $1 \times$ ₹ 10.50 + $4 \times$ ₹ 15.25
         = ₹ 10.50 + ₹ 61 = ₹ 71.5
For John,
Cost of 2 packs of pencils + 2 packs of pens
         = $2 \times$ ₹ 10.50 + $2 \times$ ₹ 15.25
         = ₹ 21 + ₹ 30.5 = ₹ 51.5
So, more money spent by Carol than John
         = ₹ 71.5 − ₹ 51.5 = ₹ 20

24. *(c)* Number of shirts Gabriella wants to buy = 10
Cost of one shirt = ₹ 200
So, cost of 10 such shirts = ₹ 200 × 10 = ₹ 2000
Discount on buying 2 shirts = ₹ 100
Discount on buying 10 shirts = ₹ 100 × (10 ÷ 2)
$$= ₹ 100 × 5 = ₹ 500$$
So, total money paid by Gabriella
$$= ₹ 2000 − ₹ 500$$
$$= ₹ 1500$$

Chapter 7 : Time and Calendar

1. *(a)* Current time shown by the clock
$$= 8 : 15\,am$$
Minutes later when the prayer will hold
$$= 15\,min$$
So, Time when the prayer will hold
$$= 8 : 15\,am + 15\,min = 8 : 30\,am$$

2. *(d)* In each time the minute hand of the given clock is jumping 5 min ahead.
The hour hand of the given clock is jumping 1 h ahead.
So, the missing time = 2 h 20 min + 1 h 5 min
$$= 3\,h\,25\,min$$
$$= 3 : 25$$

3. *(c)* Luisy started cooking the cake at the time
$$= 1 : 25 = 1\,h\,25\,min$$
Time taken to bake the cake = 150 min
$$= 120\,min + 30\,min$$
$$= 2\,h\,30\,min \qquad [∵ 1\,h = 60\,min]$$
So, the time when Luisy's cake will be ready
$$= 1\,h\,25\,min + 2\,h\,30\,min$$
$$= 3\,h\,55\,min = 3 : 55$$

4. *(d)* Given, minute hand is on 7.
So, number of min = 7 × 5 = 35 min
The h hand is between 7 and 8.
So, the time is 7 h 35 min = 7 : 35 am

5. *(c)* The time at which 1st train will pass = 5 : 05
Time when 2nd train will pass = 5 : 20
Elapsed time = 5 h 20 min − 5 h 5 min = 15 min
So, missing time = 5 : 35 + 15 min
$$= 5\,h\,35\,min + 15\,min$$
$$= 5\,h\,50\,min$$

6. *(b)* Linda left home at the time = 11 : 00 am
Time spent in walking to Staley's house = 15 min
Time spent at Staley's house = 2 h 15 min
Time spent in coming back to home = 15 min
So, total time taken
$$= 15\,min + 2\,h\,15\,min + 15\,min$$
$$= 2\,h\,45\,min$$

∴ Time when Linda arrived back to home
$$= 11 : 00\,am + 2\,h\,45\,min$$
$$= 11\,h\,0\,min + 2\,h\,45\,min$$
$$= 1 : 45\,pm = Quarter\ to\ 2$$

7. *(b)* Richard and Lisa should reach the shopping mall at 4:45 pm
∴ But he reach 15 min earlier.
i.e., 4:30 pm
Lisa is half an h late so, she reached at
4 h 45 min + 30 min
i.e., 5 : 15 pm.
∴ Richard have to wait for Lisa for
$$= 5\,h\,15\,min − 4\,h\,30\,min = 45\,min$$

8. *(c)* As we know,
1 week = 7 days.
(1 × 9) weeks = (9 × 7) days
9 weeks = 63 days.
In question we have 67 days.
∴ 9 weeks covers 63 days.
Remaining days = 67 − 63 = 4 days
So, in option (c) 9 weeks 4 days is equivalent to 67 days.

9. *(c)* Age of Robin's sister = 8 weeks
$$= (8 × 7)\ days = 56\ days$$
$$[∵ 1\ week = 7\ days]$$
Age of his friend's sister
$$= 6\ weeks\ 10\ days$$
$$= (6 × 7)\ days + 10\ days$$
$$[∵ 1\ week = 7\ days]$$
$$= 42\ days + 10\ days = 52\ days$$
∴ Number of days Robin's sister is older than his friend's sister
$$= 56\ days − 52\ days = 4\ days$$

10. *(d)* 1. 21 days
Number of days in 1 week = 7 days
Number of days in 3 weeks = 7 × 3 = 21 days

2. Friday
Correct sequence →

Five days before Wednesday is given below

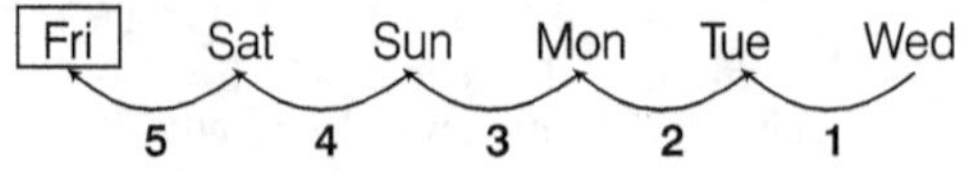

3. 28 days
Number of days in February in an ordinary year = 28

4. Saturday

   3 days before Tuesday is given below:

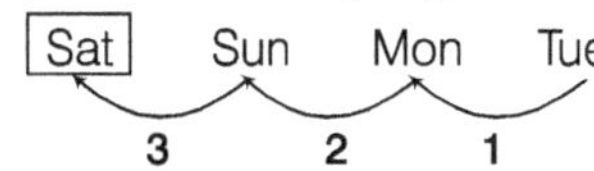

   So, today is Saturday.

   $\therefore$ 1 → D,   2 → B,   3 → A,   4 → E

   Hence, option (d) is correct.

11. (c) Number of days after which Jane will come back = 2 days

   We know that,

   $$1 \text{ day} = 24 \text{ h}$$

   So, $2 \text{ days} = (2 \times 24) \text{ h} = 48 \text{ h}$

   So, Jane will come after 48 h.

12. (b) Today's date is 8th August.

   Number of Saturday after 8th August

   $$= 3 \,(\text{i.e., 15th, 22th and 29th})$$

   So, Ralph and Sammi will meet 3 times after 8th August.

13. (d) Total number of days in month August = 31

   Number of Sundays in August = 4

   $\therefore$ One holiday is of Independence day i.e.,

   $$= 15 \text{ August}$$

   Total holidays = 4 + 1 = 5 days

   $\therefore$ Total working days for Niharika is

   $$= \text{Total number of days}$$
   $$\qquad - \text{Total holiday in August}$$
   $$= 31 - 5$$

   So, working days for Niharika = 26 days.

14. (d) A dinosaur grows 1m each day or 7m each week.

   A Gorilla grows 3m each week.

   In 3 week,

   A dinosaur grows = 7m × 3 = 21m

   A Gorilla grows = 3m × 3 = 9m

   So, a dinosaur grows 12 m more than Gorilla in 3 weeks.

15. (a) 1. False,

   The short hand of the clock is called the h hand.

   2. True,

   The hand takes 12 h to complete one round.

   3. False,

   $\because$ 1 min = 60 sec

   $\therefore$ 30 min = 30 × 60 = 1800 sec

4. False,

   7 months have 31 days in an year namely, January, March, May, July, August, October and December.

16. (b) We know that, February has 29 days in a leap year.

   Also, every leap year comes after 4 yr.

   So, if 2000 was a leap year, then the other leap years are as follow

   $$2004, 2008, 2012, 2016$$

   It is 2013 now, so after 3 yr a leap year will come, i.e., 2016.

   Therefore, she can celebrate her sister's birthday after 3 yr.

17. (d) Arrival time at stadium = 8 : 30 am

   Departure time from stadium = 10 : 20 am

   Duration of time spent in stadium

   $$= 10 : 20 \text{ am} - 8 : 30 \text{ am}$$
   $$= 10 \text{ h } 20 \text{ min} - 8 \text{ h } 30 \text{ min}$$
   $$= 1 \text{ h } 50 \text{ min}$$

18. (a) Arrival time at Nehru Planetarium

   $$= 12 : 15 \text{ pm}$$

   Time stayed at Nehru Planetarium = 2h 15 min

   So, departure time = 12 : 15 pm + 2h 15 min

   $$= 12 \text{h } 15 \text{ min} + 2 \text{ h } 15 \text{ min}$$
   $$= 2 : 30 \text{ pm}$$

19. (b) Time at which the first train arrives

   $$= 7 : 10 \text{ am}$$
   $$= 7 \text{ h } 10 \text{ min}$$

   Minutes later the train will arrives

   $$= 40 \text{ min}$$

   So, time at which the fourth train will arrive

   $$= (3 \times 40) \text{ min later}$$
   $$= 120 \text{ min later}$$
   $$= 2 \text{h} \qquad [\because 1 \text{ h} = 60 \text{ min}]$$

   So, the fourth train will arrive at

   $$= 7 \text{ h } 10 \text{ min} + 2 \text{h}$$
   $$= 9 \text{ h } 10 \text{ min} = 9 : 10 \text{ am}$$

20. (d) We know,

   $$3 \text{ weeks} = (3 \times 7) \text{ days} \qquad [\because 1 \text{ week} = 7 \text{ days}]$$
   $$= 21 \text{ days}$$

   So, 3 weeks and 3 days

   $$= 21 \text{ days} + 3 \text{ days} = 24 \text{ days}$$

   Date marked = 16th June

   So, 24 days after 16th June = 10 th July

Chapter 8 : Shapes

1. *(c)* From the options, we know that only a coin has curve edge.

2. *(c)* (a) Cylinder   3D
(b) Cube   3D
(c) Triangle   2D
(d) Cone   3D
Only triangle is 2D. So, it is different from others.

3. *(d)* In option (d) a birthday cap is the best example of a cone.

4. *(d)* With the help of base of the figure Q and figure R, Raman can draw a circle.
i.e., Q → Soft drink can and R → Cone.
Both have a curved edges.

5. *(d)* The given figure can be labelled as shown below:

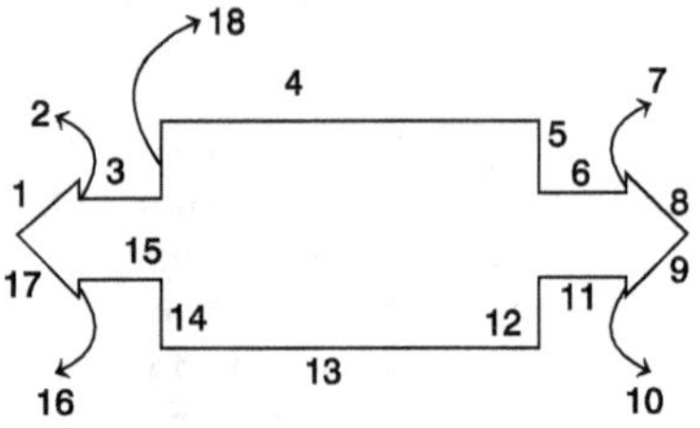

Hence, we need 18 line segments to make given figure.

6. *(b)*

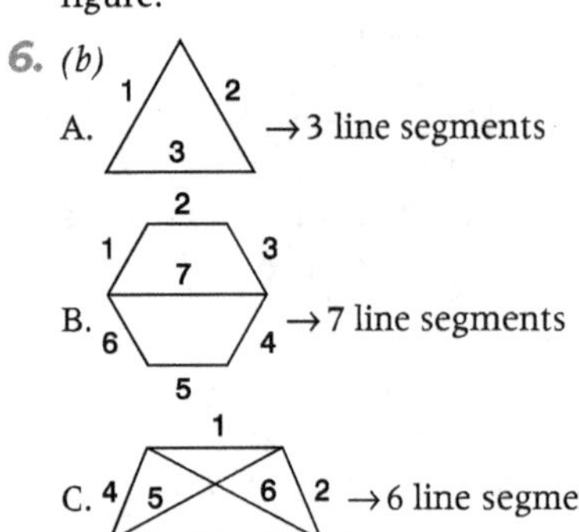

A. → 3 line segments

B. → 7 line segments

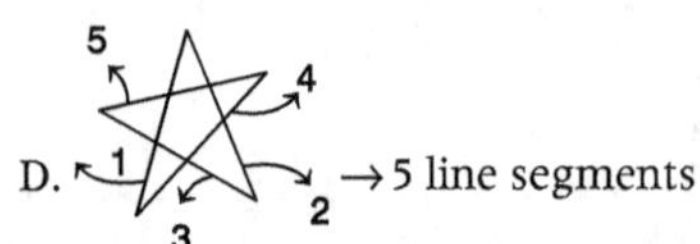

C. → 6 line segments

D. → 5 line segments

So, A → 2; B → 4; C → 1; D → 3.
Hence, option (b) is correct.

7. *(d)*

Students	Number of Squares	Number of Circles
Micheal	0	2
George	0	3
Karen	4	2
Kim	2	2

So, Karen drew the correct figure.

8. *(a)* In the given picture only triangles are in equal size.

9. *(c)*

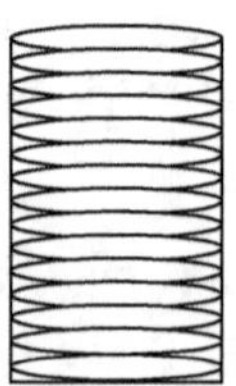

Hence, option (c) is correct.

10. *(a)* 1 Square have 4 corners.
1 Triangle has 3 corners.
Now, 4 square have = (4 × 4) corners.
= 16 corners.
3 triangles have = (3 × 3) corners
= 9 corners.
So, total numbers of corners
= 4 squares's corners
+ 3 triangle's corners
= 16 + 9 = 25

11. *(c)*

Monty placed 15 coins of ten rupee coin, exactly one on the others.
He observed carefully that a shape of cylinder is formed by such an arrangement.

12. *(d)* To walk around the given triangle squirrel have to move start point to end point and then end point to start point.

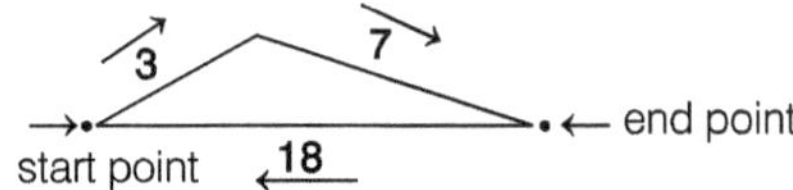

So, distance covered by squirrel
$$= 3 + 7 + 18 = 28$$

13. *(d)*

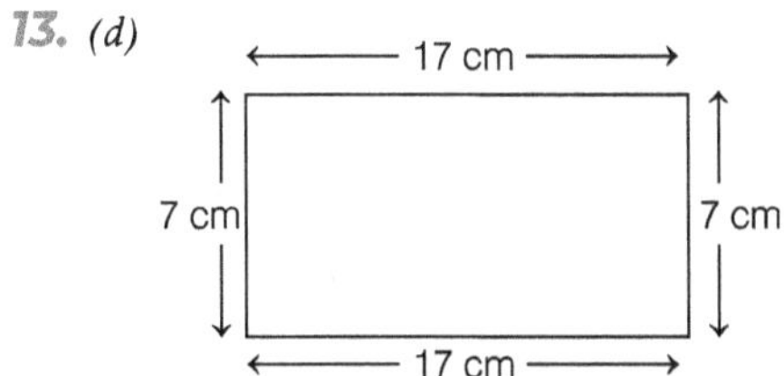

Sum of length of board made by jack
$$= 7 + 17 + 7 + 17 = 48 \text{ cm}$$

14. *(b)*

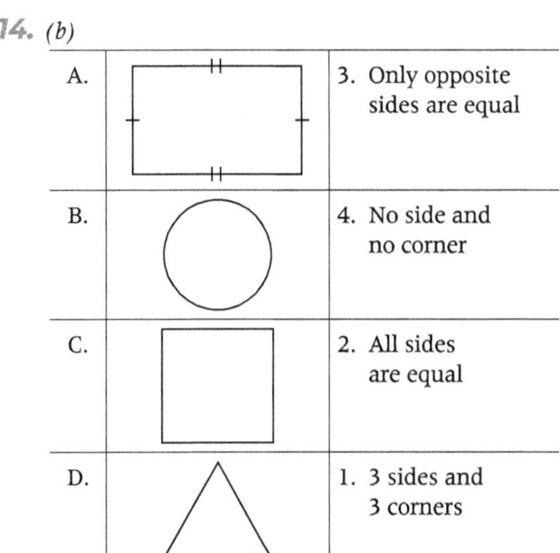

A.		3. Only opposite sides are equal
B.		4. No side and no corner
C.		2. All sides are equal
D.		1. 3 sides and 3 corners

So, A → 3; B → 4; C → 2; D → 1.
Hence, option (b) is correct.

15. *(c)* 1. A cuboid has <u>12</u> number of edges.
2. A cylinder has <u>3</u> number of faces.
3. A cone has <u>1</u> number of vertices.
4. A cube has <u>8</u> number of vertices.
∴ 1 → E, 2 → F, 3 → B, 4 → C
Hence, option (c) is correct.

16. *(a)* 1. False, a cuboid has 0 curved edges.
2. False, a cube has 12 edges.
3. False, a cone has 2 faces.
4. False, a cylinder has 2 edges.
Hence, option (a) is correct.

17. *(c)* • Made up of different shapes, i.e., square and semi-circles.
• It has 4 semi-circles.
• It has 1 square.

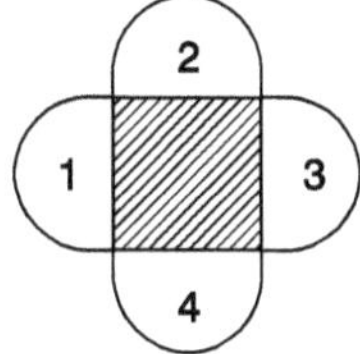

⇒ Shaded part is a square and 1, 2, 3, 4 is the semi-circles.

18. *(d)* According to the question,

Football ground

Sum of all the sides = 72 m
Let the side be x m.
Now, Sum of all sides = $x + x + x + x = 4x$
(∵ All 4 sides are equal in square)
⇒ $4x = 72$
So, $x = 72 ÷ 4$, $x = 18$ = side of field.
∴ The ground is of sides = 18 m
So, sum of two sides = 18 m + 18 m = 36 m

19. *(c)* Number of faces in the penstand has = 7

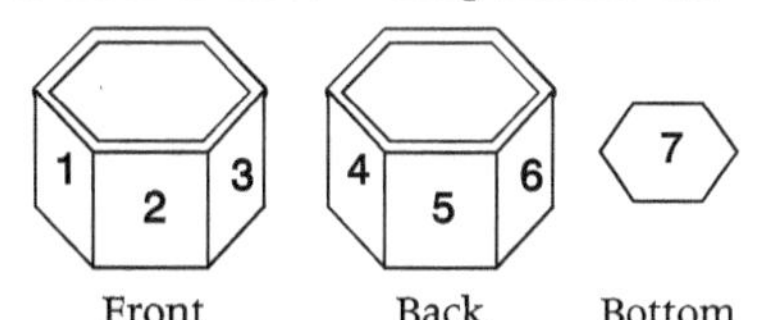

So, Ria must have used 7 colours.

20. *(d)* According to the clues, X represent properties of cuboid.
Y represent properties of cube.
Z represent properties of cylinder.
Hence, option (d) is correct.

Chapter 9 : Patterns and Symmetry

1. *(d)* The pattern of frames is ABCDEABCDE AB...
Where,

$$A = \boxed{} , B = \boxed{} , C = \boxed{} , D = \triangle , E = \triangle$$

So, the next three terms will be CDE, i.e.,

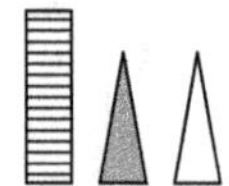

2. *(b)* In the given pattern there are increment in number of lines from first figure to second figure. So term in option (b) will complete the pattern.

3. *(a)* According to the given pattern, we have

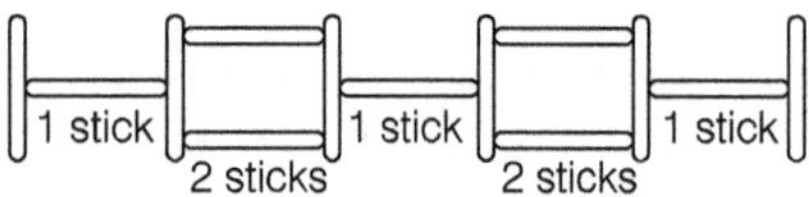

So, option (a) will be the next part of the pattern.

4. *(d)* The pattern of the pictures is based on the number of wheels each vehicle has

1st vehicle → 1

2nd vehicle → 2

4th vehicle → 4

So, the 3rd vehicle must have three wheels. Therefore, option (d) is correct.

5. *(c)* The pattern made by Grini follows the rule

$$a\,A\,a\,b\,B\,b\,c\,C\,c$$

where,

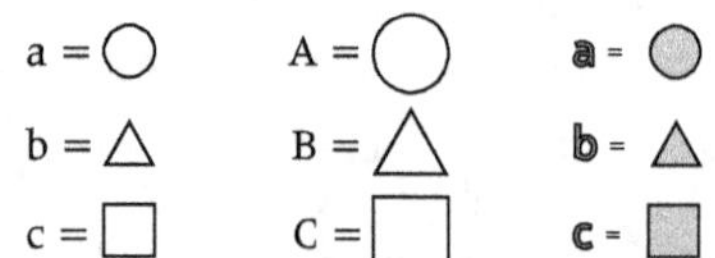

So, continuing the pattern, the next four terms will be

6. *(b)* The pattern followed by Ronit to paint the mat is ABC ABC ABC ...

where,

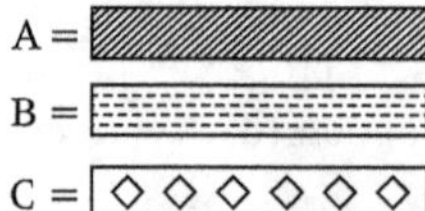

So, the next three patterns will be

B = ...
C = ...
A = ...

7. *(d)* The sequence of colours is A B C D A B C D where, A = red, B = blue, C = yellow, D = green

So, the missing colour is green.

Now, the sequence of shape is Circle, Square, Triangle, Square, Circle, Square,

Triangle, Square

So, the missing button will be a green square.

8. *(c)* The pattern followed by the given shapes is

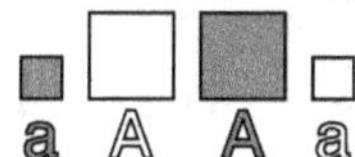

The pattern followed by each option is

(a) a A A a a A A ⋯ (b) A a a A a a A ⋯

(c) a A A a a A A ⋯

So, option (c) follows the same pattern.

9. *(c)* The border made by Dakshan follows the pattern

$$A\,B\,\forall\,C$$

Now, each block follows the pattern as

$$1 \longrightarrow A\,B\,\forall\,C$$
$$2 \longrightarrow A\,B\,\forall\,C$$
$$3 \longrightarrow \forall\,B\,A\,C$$
$$4 \longrightarrow A\,B\,\forall\,C$$

So, block 3 is not correct.

10. *(c)* Number of books is increasing by one from left to right box. So, the correct option is (c).

In which sharpner is increasing by one from left to right.

11. *(c)* Number of leaves is decreasing by 2 from going left to right.

So, correct option is (c).

Figure 1 → 8 leaves

Figure 2 → 6 leaves

Figure 3 → 4 leaves

Figure 4 → 2 leaves

12. *(d)* Number of triangles is decreasing from going boxes left to right.

Box 1 → 8

Box 2 → 6

Box 3 → 4

Box 4 ⇒ 2

Number of stars is increasing from going boxes left to right.

Box 1 → 2

Box 2 → 4

Box 3 → 6

Box 4 ⇒ 8

Hence, option (d) will be the next pattern.

13. *(c)* The pattern of shapes follows the rule as shown below:

Number of triangles in 1st figure = 3

Number of triangles in 2nd figure = 3 + 3 = 6

Number of triangles in 3rd figure = 6 + 3 = 9
Number of triangles in 4th figure = 9 + 3 = 12
So, each term is 3 more than the last one,
i.e.,

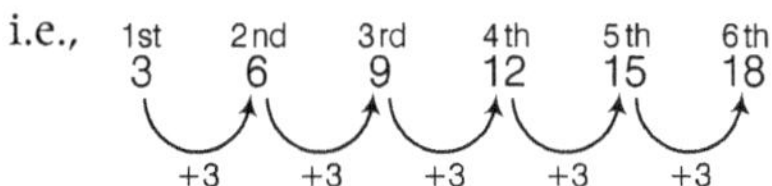

Therefore, 6th figure will have 18 triangles.
So, the given statement in option (c) is correct.

14. *(d)* We have the following pattern of dots in each ladybug:
1 year old ladybug has 3 dots.
2 years old ladybug has 5 dots.
3 years old ladybug has 7 dots.
So, the pattern is as follows

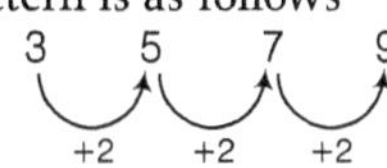

Each time dots are 2 more than the last one.
So, 4 yr old ladybug will have
= 7 + 2 = 9 dots.

15. *(d)* The number pattern made by Cameron is

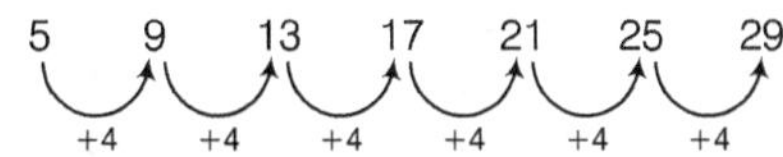

Here, each term is 4 more than the last one.
The pattern in each option is as shown below:

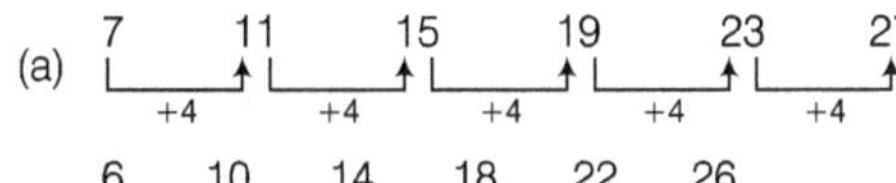

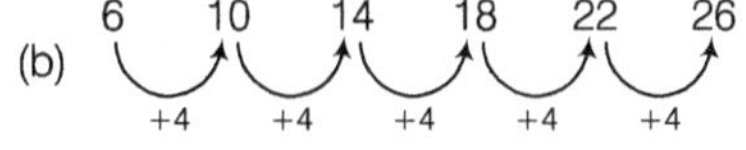

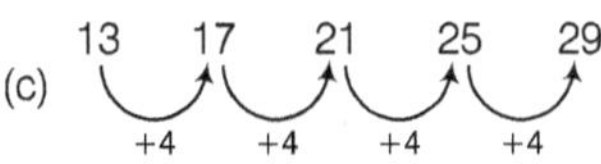

So, all follow the same pattern.

16. *(d)* The pattern is as follows:

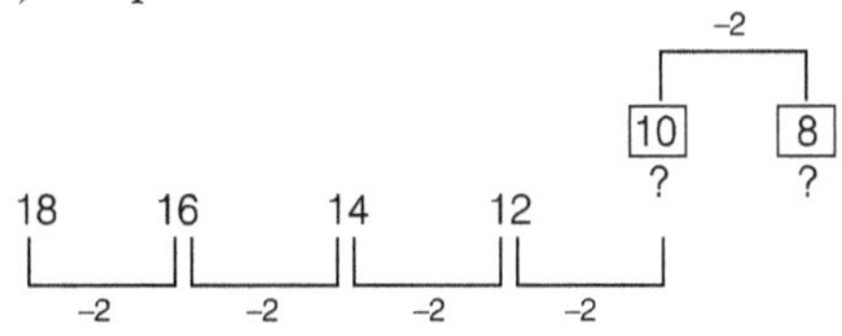

For obtaining the next term subtract 2 from the previous term.

17. *(a)* The pattern is as follows:
In first figure, 14 + 6 = 20
In second figure, 184 + 16 = 200
In third figure, 248 + 12 = 260
Hence, option (a) is correct.

18. *(b)* Top view of car is as follows:

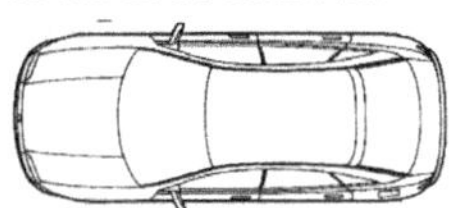

Hence, option (b) is correct.

19. *(d)* Only option (d) 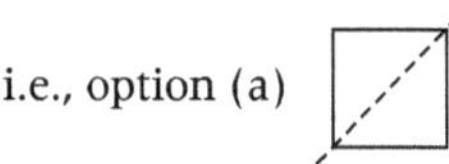 is symmetrical about the dashed line.

20. *(d)* Only option (d) is not symmetrical about the dashed line.

i.e.,

21. *(a)* Except option (a) all the unsymmetrical.

i.e., option (a)

22. *(a)* The pattern following in question is Anti-clockwise i.e., (opposite the direction in which clock revolve).
Hence, option (a) is following the required pattern.

23. *(b)* The pattern followed by
(A) △□○○□ △△□○ ···
$\qquad$ = X Y Z Z Y X X Y Z...
(B) 123 ㄴㄥㄷ 123 ···
$\qquad$ = ABD DBA ABD ···
(C) ▨◙▲▨▨◙◙▲▲ ···
$\qquad$ = PQR PPQ QRR...
(D) 123 1123 1223 = ABC AABC ABBC...
∴ A → 3, B → 4, C → 2, D → 1
Hence, option (b) is correct.

24. *(b)* The cat starts from 7 m mark and jumps 4 m everytime.
So, the pattern followed by the cat is

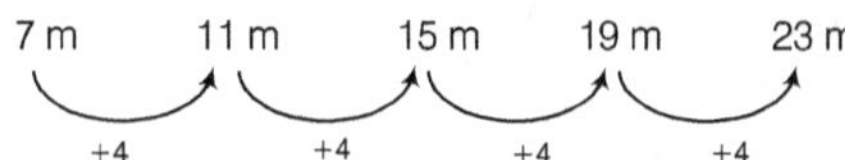

The mouse is at 23 m mark, so the cat needs to jump 4 times to reach the mouse.

25. *(a)*
1. False,
Top view and side view of a cuboid are different.

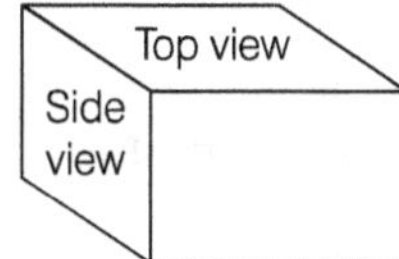

2. True,

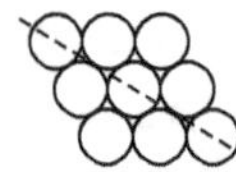

3. False,

All letters can be divided into mirror halves.
4. False, it is the side view of an umbrella.
Hence option (a) is correct.

Chapter 10 : Data Handling

1. (b) Number of children who choose Road trip
= 4.
Number of children chosen River boating = 4
So, number of children chosen road trip is equal
to number of children chosen River boating.

2. (a) Number of students chosen Amusement
park = 5
Number of students chosen Camping = 2
Difference = students chosen Amusement park
– students chosen camping
= 5 – 2 = 3

3. (d) Number of pen bought by the four children
together = Pen bought by Madhav + Pen bought
by Achyut + Pen bought by Krishna + Pen
bought by Govind = 20 + 80 + 30 + 40
[∵ each ✏ stands for 10 pens]
= 170

4. (a) Number of pen bought by Govind = 40
[∵ each ✏ stands for 10 pens]

Given, cost of each pen = ₹ 10
So, total cost of all pens = Number of pens
bought × cost of each pen = 40 × 10 = ₹ 400

5. (d) Number of ice-creams Nisha has 30.
Number of ice-creams Ravi has 60.
So, Ravi has twice ice-creams as Nisha has.

6. (b) Total number of ice-creams bought by
students together =
Number of ice-creams Rohit bought
+ Number of ice-creams Preeti bought
+ Number of ice-creams Ravi bought
+ Number of ice-creams Nisha bought
+ Number of ice-creams Anjali bought.
= 50 + 90 + 60 + 30 + 70 = 300

7. (c) Money he spend on books = ₹ 90
After not buying the books, he save ₹ 90.

8. (d) Money spend on books = ₹ 90
Money spend on bus fare = ₹ 55
So, amount of money more spend on books than
on bus fare = Money spend of books
– Money spend on bus fare
= ₹ 90 – ₹ 55 = ₹ 35

9. (a) Maximum number of bags of popcorn sold
on = Thursday
Minimum number of bags of popcorn sold on
= Wednesday.
So, required difference = 585 – 529 = 56

10. (b) Total number of bags sold on Wednesday
and Saturday together = Number of bags sold on
Wednesday + Number of bags sold on Saturday
= 529 + 552 = 1081

11. (b) Highest marks = 56
Lowest marks = 32
So, sum = Highest marks + Lowest marks
= 56 + 32 = 88

12. (d) The ascending order of the marks obtained
by 7 students is
32 < 36 < 45 < 49 < 50 < 53 < 56.
Thus, 53 is the second highest marks.
So, David got the second highest marks.

13. (d) Total number of children who visited the zoo
= 80
Number of children who voted animals other
than panther = 12 + 25 + 18 + 14 = 69
So, the number of children who voted for
panther = 80 – 69 = 11

14. (c) According to the bar graph, the marks of
friends in descending order is as follows:
Lovely > Rim > Ken > Jill > Ron
So, the friends are standing in the order
Lovely, Rim, Ken, Jill, Ron.
Hence, option (c) is correct.

15. (c) Table showing number of each type of car

Types of cars	SUV	Sedan	Hatch back	Sports car	Micro car	Minivan
Number	36	24	32	20	28	8

So, total number of cars parked in Kratikas
colony = 36 + 24 + 32 + 20 + 28 + 8 = 148

16. (c) Using the table in Q. No. 15.
Maximum number of cars parked = 36
Minimum number of cars parked = 8
So, required difference = 36 – 8 = 28

17. *(d)* We have, each  = 2 dresses

Number of purple coloured dress = $5 \times 2 = 10$
So, 8 less than number of purple
coloured dress = $10 - 8 = 2$

Now, 1 = 2 dresses

Number of orange coloured dress, = 2

So, orange is the correct answer.

18. *(d)* The table shows the number of instruments
played by each child.

Name of children	Number of instruments
Lauren	3
Jane	2
Richard	3
Nainy	2
Yon	2

So, Lauren and Richard play more than 2
instruments.

19. *(a)* Number of boys were absent on Thursday
$$= 4 \odot = 4 \times 5$$
$$= 20$$
Number of boys were absent on Friday
$$= 5 \odot = 5 \times 5$$
$$= 25$$
So, total boys were absent on Thursday and
Friday altogether = $20 + 25 = 45$

20. *(c)* Number of students who like English
and Maths = $2 \star = 2 \times 4 = 8$
Number of students who like Maths
and Science = $3 \star = 3 \times 4 = 12$
So, total number of students who like two
subjects = $12 + 8 = 20$

21. *(d)* Since, at 10 am 10 bike were parked
So, A → 2
At 12 non 40 bikes were parked
So, B → 3
At 2 pm 60 bikes were parked
So, C → 1
At 9 am 30 bikes were parked
So, D → 4
Hence, option (d) is correct.

Practice Set 1

1. *(d)* 954 hundred = $954 \times 100 = 95400$
Given, $95400 - x = 89290$
∴ $x = 95400 - 89290 = 6110$

2. *(a)* Given, 15 children got = ₹ 11895
Then, 1 child got = $11895 \div 15 = ₹ 793$
So, 2 children got = $2 \times 793 = ₹ 1586$

3. *(b)* According to question,
Cost of 1 lollipop = ₹ 18
Cost of 6 lollipop = $18 \times 6 = ₹ 108$
Kapil spent = ₹ 120
Then, cost of 3 candies = $120 - 108 = ₹ 12$
So, cost of 1 candy = $12 \div 3 = ₹ 4$

4. *(a)* Given, 4 apples = 8 kg + 8 kg = 16 kg
So, 1 apple = $16 \div 4 = 4$ kg

5. *(d)* Total number of the squares = 30
Total number of the shaded squares = 10
So, the fraction $= \dfrac{10}{30} = \dfrac{1}{3}$

6. *(b)* Let the number be x.
Now, 3 times of 6.7 = 20.100
According to the question,
$8.439 + x = 20.100$
∴ $x = 20.100 - 8.439 = 11.661$

7. *(c)* Given, Saurabh age = 10 yr
Then, his father age = 6 times of Saurabh age
$$= 6 \times 10 = 60 \text{ yr}$$
So, his mother age = 3 yr younger than his father
$$= 60 - 3 = 57 \text{ yr}$$

8. *(a)* Total number of toffees Kartik has = 80
Total number of toffees Akash has = 70
So, the difference = $80 - 70 = 10$
Hence, 10 more toffees does Kartik has than
Akash.

9. *(a)* Web series started at = 1 : 55
Web series finished at = 4 : 25
So, the duration of web series = 4 : 25 – 1 : 55
$$= 2 \text{h } 30 \text{ min}$$

10. *(c)* $97321 + 4057 = 101378$, which has 3 hundred.

11. *(c)* $572 \times 3 \times 50 = x \times 52 \times 10$
$\Rightarrow 11 \times 52 \times 3 \times 50 = x \times 52 \times 10$
$\Rightarrow 11 \times 3 \times 52 \times 5 \times 10 = x \times 52 \times 10$

$$\Rightarrow 11 \times 3 \times 5 \times 52 \times 10 = x \times 52 \times 10$$
$$\Rightarrow \quad 33 \times 5 \times 52 \times 10 = x \times 52 \times 10$$
$$\Rightarrow \quad 165 \times 52 \times 10 = x \times 52 \times 10$$
$$\therefore \qquad\qquad x = 165$$

12. *(d)* A Book is a shape of Cuboid: P $\rightarrow$ 3

A birthday hat is a shape of Cone : Q $\rightarrow$ 1

A Black-board is a shape of Rectangle : R $\rightarrow$ 2

A Ball is a shape of Circle : S $\rightarrow$ 4

Hence, option (d) is correct.

13. *(a)* The pattern is as follows:

The 1st term has 1 stars inside the shape.

The 2nd term has 2 stars inside the shape.

The 3rd term has 3 stars inside the shape.

The 4th term has 4 stars inside the shape.

The 5th term has 5 stars inside the shape.

So, The 6th term will have 6 stars inside the shape.

Hence, option (a) is correct.

14. *(a)* Original number = 8645

New number after interchanging the digits
$$= 8465$$
So, difference = 8645 − 8465 = 180

15. *(d)* Number of bananas Taru bought
$$= 10 \, \text{dozen}$$
Number of bananas gave to his sister
$$= 4 \, \text{dozen}$$
Number of bananas left = 10 − 4 = 6 dozen

Now, number of bananas in 6 dozen
$$= 6 \times 12 = 72 \, \text{bananas}$$
Bananas used for shake = 6

So, number of bananas left = 72 − 6 = 66

16. *(b)* Individual points scored by Ben
$$= 25, 35, 60, 7$$
Total of the points scored by Ben
$$= 25 + 35 + 60 + 7 = 60 + 67 = 127$$
Individual points scored by Den
$$= 15, 45, 70, 3$$
Total of the points scored by Den
$$= 15 + 45 + 70 + 3 = 60 + 73 = 133$$
We know that, 133 > 127

So, Den won the game.

Points by which Den won over Ben
$$= 133 - 127 = 6$$

17. *(b)* Packets bought in June and July = 122

Total number of days in both months
$$= 30 + 31 = 61$$
Packets bought in 1 day = 122 ÷ 61 = 2

So, Packets bought in June = 30 × 2 = 60

18. *(b)* Total amount paid by Sonu and Monu together = ₹ 1200

Given, they paid equal amount for jeans.

Amount paid by each = ₹ 1200 ÷ 2 = ₹ 600

Hence, option (b) is correct.

19. *(a)* Given, ladder height = 7 m 50 cm

Navya climbed at ladder = 4 m 25 cm

So, left ladder height need to climb to reach the top = 7 m 50 cm − 4 m 25 cm = 3 m 25 cm

20. *(b)* Given, 1 icon = 3 person's favourite

So, 5 × 3 person's favourite = 5 × 1 icon

$\Rightarrow$ 15 person's favourite = 5 icons

The animal having 5 icons is lions.

So, the lion is liked by 15 people.

21. *(a)* The number of people who like the category of other animals
$$= 6 \times 3 = 18$$
6 more number of people than the one who like other animal
$$= 18 + 6 = 24$$
Now, 1 icon = 3 person's favourite

$\therefore$ 8 icons = 8 × 3 = 24 person's favourite

So, the animal liked by 24 person's is horse.

22. *(a)* The given pattern is as follows:

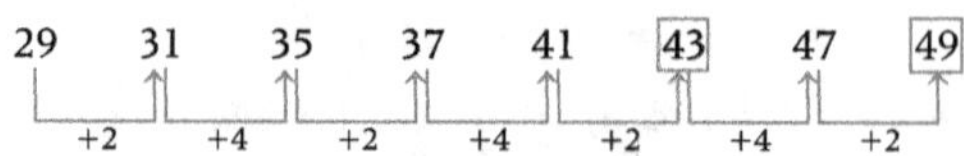

So, the missing number in the pattern are: 43, 49.

23. *(d)* Given, Anshu's height = 159 cm

Stuti's height = 159 − 6 = 153 cm

Karishma's height is same as Stuti's height
$$= 153 \, \text{cm}$$
So, Shubhi's height will be
$$= 153 + 16 = 169 \, \text{cm}$$

24. *(c)* As we know, [1 h = 60 min]

Minutes given in question = 350 min

$\therefore$ 5 h = 5 × 60 = 300 min

Remaining min = 350 min − 300 min = 50 min

i.e. 5 h 50 min

25. *(d)* Considering option (d), only cylinder is the figure which has 3 faces.

26. *(b)* According to the given calendar, 5th Sunday date in November, 2020 is November 29.

27. *(a)* In the given picture, there are 5 cubes in all.

So, the fraction $= \dfrac{5}{20}$

Hence, option (a) is correct.

28. *(b)* $4.3 \times 6 \times 0.25 = 4.3 \times (6 \times 0.25)$

$$= 4.3 \times 1.5 = 6.45$$

29. *(a)* Considering all options:

(a) 4.3 m < 5.2 m < 5.22 m < 6 m

(b) 3.33 L > 0.5 L < 2.2 L > 0.75 L

(c) 0.9 kg < 1.2 kg < 2.35 kg > 1.5 kg

So, the order given in option (a) shows the correct ascending order.

Hence, option (a) is correct.

30. *(b)* The given pattern is as follows:

$$10 \times 15 = 150$$
$$6 \times 25 = 150$$
$$5 \times 30 = 150$$
$$2 \times A = 150$$
$$\Rightarrow \qquad A = 150 \div 2$$
$$\therefore \qquad A = 75$$

31. *(c)* Harsh sold 125 burgers and 90 spring rolls.

Nitin sold = 125 burgers and 90 spring rolls − 20 burgers and 10 spring rolls

= 105 burgers and 80 spring rolls

Thus, total burgers sold

$$= 125 + 105 = 230$$

and total spring rolls sold

$$= 90 + 80 = 170$$

32. *(a)* Ending time of each tour is

Bus	Departure time	End time
Red coach	9 : 45 am	2 : 00 pm
Blue coach	11 : 25 am	3 : 40 pm
Green coach	1 : 40 pm	5 : 55 pm
Yellow coach	3 : 15 pm	7 : 30 pm
Orange coach	4 : 00 pm	8 : 15 pm

So, they can take blue coach bus for the tour.

33. *(c)* Given, total distance travelled = 1028 km

Distance travelled by bus $= \dfrac{1028}{2} = 514$ km

Distance left = 1028 − 514 = 514 km

Distance travelled by car $= \dfrac{514}{2} = 257$ km

So, distance travelled by walking
$$= 514 - 257 = 257 \text{ km}$$

34. *(d)* Weight of 5 squares = 15 kg

Weight of 1 square = 15 ÷ 5 = 3 kg

Weight of 2 squares = 2 × 3 = 6 kg

Given, weight of 2 squares and 1 cylinder
$$= 11 \text{ kg}$$

$\therefore$ Weight of 1 cylinder = 11 − 6 = 5 kg

So, weight of 2 cylinder = 2 × 5 = 10 kg

35. *(a)* Alka amount = ₹ 375 + ₹ 590 + ₹ 460
$$= ₹ 1425$$
Anubhav amount = ₹ 185 + ₹ 470 + ₹ 745
$$= ₹ 1400$$
Sunny amount = ₹ 180 + ₹ 690 + ₹ 466
$$= ₹ 1336$$
Nisha amount = ₹ 550 + ₹ 425 + ₹ 375
$$= ₹ 1350$$
Astha = ₹ 315 + ₹ 766 + ₹ 240
$$= ₹ 1321$$
Akshat = ₹ 745 + ₹ 355 + ₹ 145
$$= 1245$$

Now, considering option (a).

1. Akshat spent the least amount.

2. Astha spent ₹ 1321 on shopping.

3. Sunny spent ₹ 1336 on shopping.

4. Alka spent the most amount.

Hence, option (a) is correct.

Practice Set 2

1. *(c)* We have,

Length of the mirror $= 15$ buttons

$$3 \text{ button} = 1 \text{ safety pin}$$

So,　$5 \times 3 \text{ buttons} = 5 \times 1 \text{ safety pins}$

$$15 \text{ buttons} = 5 \text{ safety pins}$$

So, length of mirror $= 5$ safety pins

2. *(b)* Given,

$$A \xrightarrow{4219} \text{Hundred's place}$$
$$B \xrightarrow{3246} \text{Hundred's place}$$
$$C \xrightarrow{1421} \text{Ten's place}$$
$$D \xrightarrow{5219} \text{Hundred's place}$$

So, A, B and D streets have 2 in the hundred's place.

3. *(c)* The model shows a flat rectangular top.

Only figure in option (c) has a flat rectangular top.

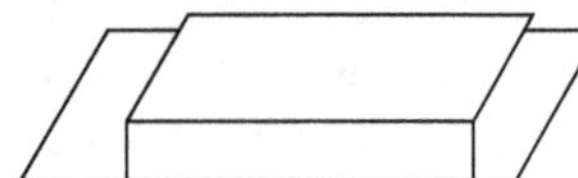

So, option (c) is correct.

4. *(b)*

Number said by friends	Number said by Romela
5	$5 \times 4 = 20$
9	$9 \times 4 = 36$
12	$12 \times 4 = 48$

So, the number Romela says is 4 times the number her friends said.

When her friend said 29, Romela will say $29 \times 4 = 116$

5. *(d)* Total distance covered by Elena in two days $= 12 \text{ km}$

Distance covered on first day

$$= \frac{5}{6} \text{ of total distance}$$

$$= \frac{5}{6} \times 12 = \frac{60}{6} = 10 \text{ km}$$

So, remaining distance covered on second day

$$= 12 - 10 \text{ km} = 2 \text{ km}$$

6. *(c)* Number of stars in 1st figure $= 4$

Number of stars in 2nd figure $= 7 = 4 + 3$

Number of stars in 3rd figure $= 10 = 7 + 3$

Each figure has 3 more stars than the previous figure.

So, the pattern is

$$4, \ 7, \ 10, \ 13, \ 16, \ 19, \ 22, \ 25, \ 28, \ 31 \ +3$$

Hence, the 9th figure will have 28 number of stars.

7. *(c)* Number of apple slices on the tray $= 40$

Number of pear slices on the tray $= 12$ less than the number of slices of apple.

So, $\square = 40 - 12$

Hence, option (c) is correct.

8. *(c)* Weight of glass $= 100 \text{ g}$

Weight of glass and cup $= 150 \text{ g}$

i.e.　　　　glass $+$ cup $= 150 \text{ g}$

So, Weight of cup

$$= 150 \text{ g} - \text{Weight of glass}$$

$$= 150 \text{ g} - 100 \text{ g} = 50 \text{ g}$$

9. *(b)* Total number of cupcakes $= 134$

Number of cupcakes in one box $= 11$

Number of boxes required $= 134 \div 11$

```
11)134(12
   11
   24
   22
    2  = Remainder
```

So, number of boxes $= 12$ and

Number of cupcakes left $= 2$

10. *(b)* Number of wheels in a bicycle $= 2$

Number of wheels in a tricycle $= 3$

Total wheels counted by Elle $= 13$

Consider each option, the total number of wheels are

(a) $3 \times 2 + 2 \times 3 = 6 + 6 = 12$

(b) $5 \times 2 + 1 \times 3 = 10 + 3 = 13$

(c) $4 \times 2 + 1 \times 3 = 8 + 3 = 11$

(d) $3 \times 2 + 4 \times 3 = 6 + 12 = 18$

So, option (b) is correct.

11. *(c)* The given digits are

$$\boxed{5}\quad\boxed{6}\quad\boxed{3}$$

The numbers that can be formed using 3 digits are

3 at hundred's place 356, 365

5 at hundred's place 536, 563

6 at hundred's place 635, 653

So, the numbers formed are

365, 356, 635, 653, 536, 563

12. *(c)* Given, sum of two-digit number. Sum of one-digit number.

So, we get $\ast = 10$

$\therefore \qquad \ast = 10 \div 2 = 5$

and $\qquad 2\,\text{☼} = 8$

$\therefore \qquad \text{☼} = 8 \div 2 = 4$

Also, $\quad ✓ + \ast = 11$

So, $\qquad ✓ = 11 - \ast$

$\qquad\qquad = 11 - 5$

$\qquad\qquad ✓ = 6$

Now,

So, we get $46 - \bigstar\ast = 21$

$\therefore \qquad \bigstar\ast = 46 - 21$

$\qquad\qquad = 25$

$\therefore \qquad \bigstar = 2$

13. *(a)* Money collected for Girl's education charity

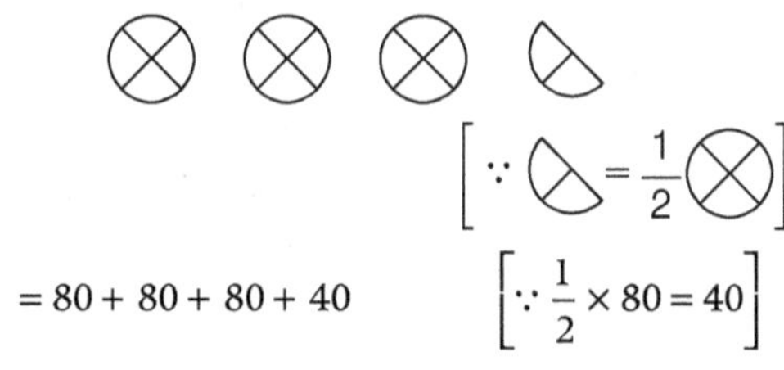

$$\left[\because \bigotimes = \frac{1}{2}\bigotimes\right]$$

$= 80 + 80 + 80 + 40 \qquad \left[\because \frac{1}{2} \times 80 = 40\right]$

$= ₹\ 280$

Money collected for old age people

$= \bigotimes\ \bigotimes\ \bigotimes$

$= 80 + 80 + 20$

$$\left[\because \bigotimes = \frac{1}{4}\bigotimes \text{ i.e. } = \frac{1}{4} \times 80 = 20\right]$$

$= ₹\ 180$

So, more money collected for girl's education than old age people $= ₹\ 280 - ₹\ 180$

$\qquad\qquad\qquad\qquad = ₹\ 100$

14. *(d)* Beginning of first session $=$ July 13

Two weeks $= 2 \times 7 = 14$ days

$\qquad\qquad\qquad [\because 1 \text{ week} = 7 \text{ days}]$

So, 14 days before July 13 $=$ 29th June

[July 12, 11, 10, 9, 8, 7, 6, 5, 4, 3, 2, 1, June 30, 29]

15. *(b)* Starting date of session 3 $= 1$ August

Day on 1st day of session 3 $=$ Monday Since, First Wednesday will be on $= 3$ August

So, second Wednesday will be on

$\qquad\qquad\qquad = 3$ August $+ 7$ days

$\qquad\qquad\qquad = 10$th August

The date on which broadway show will be put on is 10th August.

16. *(c)* Number of rows $= 6$

Number of plants in one row $= 5$

So, number of plants in 6 rows $= 6 \times 5$

More plants planted in another row $= 3$

So, total number of rose plants $= (6 \times 5) + 3$

17. *(d)* According to the question,

The number formed is 2 ten thousands 4 thousands 0 hundreds 7 tens 3 ones

$= 2 \times 10000 + 4 \times 1000 + 0 \times 100 + 7 \times 10 + 3 \times 1$

$= 20000 + 4000 + 0 + 70 + 3$

$= 24073$

18. *(b)* Total number of stickers $= 9$

Number of stickers with stars $= 2$

So, fraction of stickers with stars $= \dfrac{2}{9}$

19. *(d)* The pattern of figures is

In the third term, the first figure is inserted in the second figure.
So, the 6th term will be

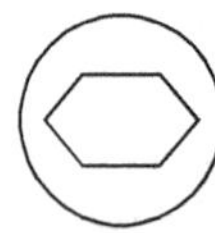

20. *(c)* Fraction of pieces Emily ate $= \dfrac{1}{5}$

Number of pieces she ate $= 15 \times \dfrac{1}{5} = 3$

Fraction of pieces Tenzen ate $= \dfrac{2}{5}$

Number of pieces Tenzen ate $= \dfrac{2}{5} \times 15 = 6$

Fraction of pieces Jaun ate $= \dfrac{1}{5}$

Number of pieces Jaun ate $= 15 \times \dfrac{1}{5} = 3$

So, number of pieces left $= 15 - (3 + 3 + 6)$
$= 15 - 12 = 3$

21. *(b)* Distance from Town Z to Town X
$= 148 + 247 = 395 \, \text{km}$

Distance from Town Y to Town W
$= 247 + 124 = 371 \, \text{km}$

So, Linda travelled more distance by 24 km
i.e. $(395 - 371) = 24 \, \text{km}$

22. *(c)* Number of triangles in the figure $= 6$

Number of rectangles in the figure $= 10$
Number of circles in the figure $= 4$
So, number of triangles is less than number of rectangles, because $6 < 10$.
So, statement (c) is true.

23. *(a)* Distance from Boston to Houstan
$= 1804 \, \text{miles}$
$= 1000 + 800 + 0 + 4$
$= 1 \times 1000 + 8 \times 100 + 0 + 4 \times 1$

$=$ One thousand eight hundred and four miles.

24. *(d)* Rent of sand castle kit for 1 h $= ₹\, 80$
Rent of sand castle kit for 3 h $= ₹\, 80 \times 3$
$= ₹\, 240$

Rent of a towel for 1 h $= ₹\, 15$
Rent of a towel for 3 h $= ₹\, 15 \times 3 = ₹\, 45$
So, total cost $= ₹\, 240 + ₹\, 45 = ₹\, 285$

25. *(a)* Total stickers bought $= 180$

Number of pokemon stickers

$= \dfrac{4}{9}$ of total stickers

$= \dfrac{4}{9} \times 180 = 80$

Remaining number of stickers $= 180 - 80$
$= 100$
So, number of spiderman stickers $= 100$

26. *(b)* According to the question,
4 balls = 2 sharpeners
So, 1 sharpener = 2 balls
Also, 4 pencils = 2 balls
$\Rightarrow$ 1 ball = 2 pencils
$\Rightarrow$ 3 balls = 6 pencils
Hence, option (b) is correct.

27. *(b)* Given, total number of girls $= 21$
Total number of boys $= 18$
Then, total students in one section $=$ Number of girls + Number of boys $= 21 + 18 = 39$
So, total students in 5 sections $= 5 \times 39 = 195$

28. *(a)* Total number of blocks $= 12$

Total number of shaded blocks $= 5$
So, the fraction
$$= \dfrac{\text{Total number of shaded blocks}}{\text{Total number of blocks}} = \dfrac{5}{12}$$

29. *(b)* Total number of stamps $= 108$
5 pupils shared 44 stamps.
Then, remaining number of stamps
$= 108 - 44 = 64$
Number of pupils who had 8 stamps each
$= 64 \div 8 = 8$

So, total number of pupils $= 5 + 8 = 13$

30. *(c)* Mayank go on a movie = 8th June

Now, total days in 2 weeks 3 days = 2 weeks + 3 days = 14 days + 3 days [∵ 1 week = 7 days]

$= 17$ days

So, the date of after 17 days $= 8 + 17$

$= 25$th June

Hence, the day of 25th June is Monday.

31. *(d)* A Dice is a shape of Cube.

A Bottle cap is a shape of Circle.

A Black board is a shape of Rectangle.

A Pencil box is a shape of Cuboid.

So, A → 3; B → 1; C → 4; D → 2

Hence, option (b) is correct.

32. *(c)* Considering all options:

(a) $5 \times 0.10 + 8 \times 0.25 + 4 \times 0.50$

$= ₹\, 0.50 + ₹\, 2 + ₹\, 2 = ₹\, 4.5$

(b) $10 \times 0.10 + 12 \times 0.25 + 1 \times 0.50$

$= ₹\, 1 + ₹\, 3 + ₹\, 0.50 = ₹\, 4.5$

(c) $10 \times 0.10 + 12 \times 0.25 + 2 \times 0.50$

$= ₹\, 1 + ₹\, 3 + ₹\, 1 = ₹\, 5$

(d) $20 \times 0.10 + 4 \times 0.25 + 3 \times 0.50$

$= ₹\, 2 + ₹\, 1 + ₹\, 1.5 = ₹\, 4.5$

So, combination given in option (c) will help Akash in buying the chocolate.

33. *(a)* Considering option (a)

(a) 2 min 5 sec $= (2 \times 60)$ sec + 5 sec

[∵ 1 min = 60 sec]

$= 120$ sec + 5 sec $= 125$ sec

So, the term given in option (a) is the same as 125 sec.

34. *(d)* Total money spent on shoes $= ₹\, 550$

Total money spent on shocks $= 80 \times 2 = ₹\, 160$

Total money spent on belt $= ₹\, 150$

Total money spent $= ₹\, 550 + ₹\, 160 + ₹\, 150$

$= ₹\, 860$

So, money left $= ₹\, 1500 - ₹\, 860 = ₹\, 640$

35. *(d)* Starting time of the first session

$= 8:15$ am

Duration of the session is 3 h 30 min.

So, end time $= 8$ h 15 min + 3 h 30 min

$= 11:45$ am